Make it Paleo II

over **175 new** grain-free recipes for the Primal Palate

Hayley Mason and Bill Staley
with Caitlin Grace Nagelson

VICTORY BELT PUBLISHING INC.
Las Vegas

First Published in 2015 by Victory Belt Publishing

ISBN: 978-1628600-59-9

Additional photography of Hayley, Bill, and Caitlin by:
    Ryan Michael White
    Kelli Ann Beavers

Cover design by:
    Bill Staley

Interior design:
    Bill Staley, Yordan Terziev, and Boryana Yordanova

Hair styling by:
    Samantha Gaiser

Makeup by:
    Hayley Mason

also by Hayley and Bill:
    Make it Paleo (2011)
    The 30 Day Guide to Paleo Cooking (2013)
    Gather: The Art of Paleo Entertaining (2013)

Printed in the U.S.A.
RRD 0115

for more recipes, visit
PrimalPalate.com

contents

To my sister

My little sister Caitlin, who would eat only white food,
hamburgers with ketchup, and plain cheese pizza as a child.
You now have a diverse palate, far greater than my own.
You are one of the most talented cooks and food stylists
I have ever had the privilege to be around.
You inspire me to be better and learn more.

Thank you for being a part of this project with us;
Bill and I are forever grateful.

—H.M.

introduction

Since we released our first cookbook, *Make it Paleo,* many changes have taken place in our lives. The biggest change is that we got married in August 2013 (finally, after writing three cookbooks together). Many people thought we were already married when we wrote *Make it Paleo,* but we had actually been together for only a little over a year.

For those of you who don't know the story, we met on the set of a music video on an icy day in March 2010. Hayley was doing the makeup for the lead singer, and Bill was playing drums in the band. Throughout the day, we had a few chances to talk. And as we talked, we discovered that we shared a passion for health and well-being, which would be ignited just a few months later when we decided to take the Paleo plunge together and start a food blog, *The Food Lovers' Primal Palate.* With blogging came a large measure of accountability: we were going to cook new food every week and share it with our readers. This turned out to be one of the most profound, life-altering decisions either of us has ever made, and we've never looked back.

In the spring of 2011, we wrote *Make it Paleo,* which was one of the very first Paleo cookbooks to be released! A couple years later, we went on to write *Gather,* an entertaining cookbook, and *The 30 Day Guide to Paleo Cooking,* a beginners' guidebook. We've been blessed to find something we enjoy doing so much that contributes not only to our own health, but to that of others as well. We've continued to grow together, as a team, and we are so grateful for this journey.

what inspired us to write this book?

It's hard for us to believe that it's been more than three years since we wrote *Make it Paleo*. That book is near and dear to our hearts for many reasons. It reminds us where this journey started for us. It challenged us to go beyond our comfort zones and put every ounce of creativity we had into a book that now helps others improve their health. *Make it Paleo* is a physical reminder of our strength as couple and our commitment to each other. That book, like every book we have written, was a labor of love. It embodies our passion and is an expression of art for us.

All artists grow and develop their craft over time. That is exactly what has happened for us since the release of *Make it Paleo* in 2011. We have evolved as recipe creators and food stylists. This book is a tribute to the original *Make it Paleo*: our first love and our first success. The big difference with this book is the addition of Hayley's sister, Caitlin. She is a trained sushi chef and one of the most inspiring cooks we know. She puts so much thought and care into the food she makes, yet it appears effortless. Not only do we have four physical pieces of work that we created as partners in everything, and now as husband and wife, but we now have a creation to share with Caitlin, too. We hope this book touches the hearts of all our readers, because it will forever be one of the most special projects we have been blessed to work on.

healing ourselves through paleo

So you've been told that the Paleo diet will make you superhuman, and all of your ailments will miraculously disappear. After thirty days, you will be left with a washboard stomach, flawless skin, and perfect blood work, and you'll be able to run at the speed of light, rid the world of all crime, and save kittens from the tallest of trees. For some people, all of those things do happen, and quickly! Well, not all of them, but you get what we're saying. We have witnessed some amazing transformations, including our own, but sometimes it takes a little more than thirty days of strict Paleo eating.

Throughout this journey, the two of us have learned so much about Paleo and also about ourselves.

hayley's story

What made me embrace the Paleo diet was that for the first time in my life, I was able to lose weight and keep it off effortlessly. I felt better both physically and emotionally than I had in my whole life—a life spent wondering why I couldn't eat the same foods my friends and family could without immediately gaining weight. Finally, I was able to feel good inside and out, and I was happy. Although aesthetics were what originally drew me to Paleo, it's not what kept me there.

The way I eat has transformed many times throughout my life, and now my main focus is health. Not only have I lost weight and gained health, but I have created wellness in my life that goes far beyond food. For me, emotional health has been a lifelong struggle; I've had severe anxiety since I was a small child. Just as someone with an autoimmune disease needs to manage his or her symptoms with nutrition, I do as well, and I've learned how diet and lifestyle influence how I feel mentally and emotionally. I've also eliminated as many toxins from our home as possible. Replacing my haircare and skincare products with natural versions has left me with flawless skin and long, thick, healthy hair.

My health journey continues as time passes. I keep learning and evolving, and that's okay.

bill's story

During the writing of *Make it Paleo* (2011), I discovered a troubling pattern of digestive issues (to put it lightly) after eating certain foods, though it was hard to tell what was making me sick. Things like coconut milk, onions, garlic, avocado, and certain fruits made my digestive tract a ticking time bomb. Hayley was doing research one day and came across a blog post about foods called FODMAPs, which essentially are fermentable carbohydrates. In my case, this intolerance turned out to be a marker of leaky gut, a condition in which the lining of the small intestine is compromised and lets larger-than-desired molecules of food through to the bloodstream. When the bloodstream sees certain chains of food that look like intruders, the whole system goes on red alert, and the intestines kick everything out. I suffered from these symptoms for almost fifteen years without knowing what was going on, but it was only during the writing of our first book that the telling pattern emerged and we were able to figure it out.

After several trips to our functional medicine doctor, we developed a plan to treat my leaky gut. I had to eliminate fermented foods from my diet in preparation for some tests that needed to be conducted. At that point, I was a serious kombucha (fermented tea) addict. To replace this daily ritual, I started drinking aloe water. Little did I know that the aloe began to heal my gut before the tests were even performed. Despite a little bit of gut healing, the tests revealed that I still showed symptoms of leaky gut, with a variety of food intolerances to go along with it. I adopted a squeaky-clean Paleo regimen, along with some supplements that my functional medicine doctor prescribed. While my progress seemed slow at first, this approach allowed my gut to fully heal in about six months, with major relief after the first four months. Even two years later, I am symptom-free!

This way of eating has transformed both of our lives. Although we continue to refine our diet as we learn more about what makes us feel our best, we are always reminded of the power of real food. We hope this book helps inspire you to start a new journey to health, or to continue on the one you've already begun.

what is the paleo diet?

Paleo is a way of eating that recalls the more natural way that human beings ate prior to the rise of highly processed modern "foods." Paleo is short for Paleolithic, and the original premise of the diet was to adhere to a list of foods that primitive peoples could have hunted or gathered before the dawn of agriculture. These are the foods that our bodies are best adapted to eating (generally speaking) from an evolutionary perspective. As you'll see after flipping through this book, though, we're not trying to re-create the foods of the Neanderthals or early humans. On the contrary, our approach to Paleo is to take the fundamental principles and put a modern culinary spin on them.

the basics of paleo

what can you eat?

The foods you should focus on eating are animals and plants. This means you can enjoy meats (beef, pork, and wild game), poultry, eggs, seafood, vegetables that grow above and below ground, fruits, and healthy fats. To get big flavors going, you can spice up those foods with natural seasonings such as herbs, spices, and salts. It's also okay to garnish those foods with nuts and seeds.

Some people wonder how much of these foods to eat. A good rule of thumb is to think of the foods' availability to early humans. Did cavemen go around snacking on bags of organic dry-roasted almonds sweetened with honey? Probably not. Early hunter-gatherers had varied diets, but the primary staples of those diets were animals and plants.

Early humans hunted for meat and gathered what plants they could (vegetables, fruits like berries, and tubers). When we build our plates, we focus on lots of colorful vegetables and animal protein, along with some fruit, and garnish with fat. This may mean cooking the food in a saturated fat or drizzling an oil-based dressing over a salad.

Occasionally, if you tolerate them well, you can enjoy some "safe starches." It's been a while since the first version of the Paleo diet went public, so it's worthwhile to note that the list of generally accepted foods has changed a bit in recent years. Many in the Paleo community have recently welcomed back white rice, white potatoes, and full-fat dairy as foods that are okay to enjoy on occasion. Some people even find that they feel better when they include these foods in their diet.

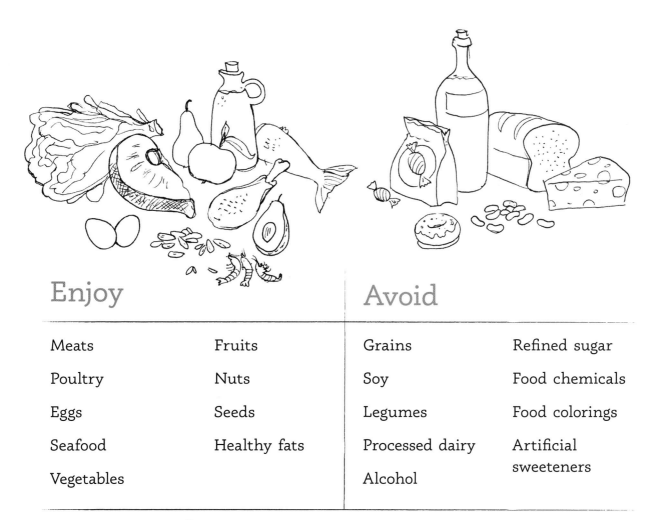

Enjoy

Meats	Fruits
Poultry	Nuts
Eggs	Seeds
Seafood	Healthy fats
Vegetables	

Avoid

Grains	Refined sugar
Soy	Food chemicals
Legumes	Food colorings
Processed dairy	Artificial sweeteners
Alcohol	

Occasional

White potatoes, white rice, full-fat dairy

but isn't white rice a processed grain? and aren't potatoes basically just starch?

Both of those statements are accurate and might confuse those who are new to Paleo. White rice is indeed a processed grain, which flies in the face of the conventional explanation of the Paleo diet being strictly grain-free. However, white rice is processed in a way that makes it more agreeable to our bodies and digestive tracts. White rice is considered an ancient grain, cultivated by humans 10,000 to 12,000 years ago.

Processing rice to remove the brown husk eliminates the part that is most irritating to our guts. The overarching theme of Paleo is to limit gut irritation and reduce inflammation, after all (not to replicate foods available to humans during a particular era). If you can handle the starch aspect of rice, then it's okay to eat it once in a while.

The same goes for white potatoes, which are part of the nightshade family of plants. Nightshades—peppers, tomatoes, and eggplant, to name a few—are plants that have defense mechanisms in their skins. These prompt an inflammatory response in some folks, which is why nightshade-free and autoimmune-friendly versions of Paleo have gained popularity in recent years. With white potatoes, removing the skins also removes the glycoalkaloids, which are the gut-irritating portions of the tuber, although this process does not make potatoes a good choice for those with severe autoimmune issues. What's left is almost purely starch (which our bodies break down as sugars). White potatoes won't help you lose weight, but they might help you replenish your glycogen stores after a grueling workout.

Other foods that you may be able to enjoy in moderation, if you tolerate them, are full-fat, grass-fed, and raw dairy. You can also enjoy grain-free or naturally sweet treats (such as those sweetened with honey, dates, or maple syrup), which you will find at the back of this book, every now and then. But don't go crazy eating "Paleo treats" just because they are included in this book. They are not a diet food. They will not help you achieve a weight-loss goal. They will, however, help you celebrate life's special moments with something sweet that others can enjoy as well. These treats are in this book to help you get back to feeling like you can live a normal life and enjoy food. Enjoying good food is one of life's wonderful treasures!

what you should avoid

Generally, you should avoid all grains, especially wheat and corn, and all soy (especially anything you know to be genetically modified). Also avoid legumes (which include peanuts), seed oils, chemical preservatives, food colorings, and artificial ingredients. These are the foods that cause inflammation in the body, promote weight gain, cause wild fluctuations in blood sugar, and have other equally unappealing side effects. Avoiding genetically modified foods (GMO) is fairly self-explanatory: there is simply not enough evidence to support that GMO foods are safe for consumption, so it's best to steer clear of them. The same goes for chemical ingredients like artificial sweeteners and food colorings.

conclusion

In the Paleo community at large, we've witnessed some big changes: as we said above, people are starting to change their stance on starches like white potatoes and white rice, as well as full-fat, grass-fed, and raw dairy and fermented dairy. Our goal with this book has been to keep the recipes free of dairy and all grains; however, we do include a few recipes that contain full-fat dairy and white potatoes. Many of these recipes list modifications for those with food intolerances.

As bloggers and authors, we feel more of a responsibility than ever to cater to those who need to follow specific types of Paleo diets to help heal a disease they may suffer from. In fact, there are many more resources available to those who need to be on a strict autoimmune protocol diet now than there were just a few years ago, including published cookbooks specifically for those who need to take even more care than those who follow the basic guidelines of the Paleo diet. We think this is a great thing for the community—so much so that we've added over a dozen special diet filters to help people search for recipes on our website, PrimalPalate.com. You can filter recipes based on autoimmune protocol needs, food allergies, preferences (like sugar-free recipes), and more.

In this book, you will find recipes marked dairy-free, nut-free, egg-free, and nightshade-free, as applicable.

This community has grown substantially since the release of our first cookbook, and it's really inspiring to watch. Multiple health-related conferences are held every year, where the numbers of educators and attendees continue to grow. There are more resources than I'm sure most people know what to do with to help keep them on track and better their health—everything from ebooks to printed cookbooks to websites and podcasts. There are meal plans and guidebooks, along with hundreds of thousands of recipes. Support can be found via Instagram, Facebook, and Twitter, and it's not focused not just on weight loss, but also on putting chronic disease into remission, boosting fertility, keeping infants and children healthy, reducing environmental toxins, improving quality of sleep, meditating, beauty and personal care, and more—a whole-life-centered way of living to optimize your well-being. We continue to educate ourselves and continue along our own journeys, all while being able to help others stay on track. It's a truly rewarding way to live, and we couldn't be more grateful.

ready to get started?

If this is your first Paleo cookbook, great—we're going to help you get started. Let's dig in and talk Paleo! If this book is on the verge of breaking your Paleo bookshelf, then you can move right on to the recipes beginning on pg 58.

all about ingredients

When you're just starting to eat Paleo, the first thing you do is look at food differently. Grocery shopping might take you a little longer because you'll pause to read the ingredients listed on the backs of the packages. Or better yet, you might start looking for food without any packaging at all. Perhaps you'll even strike up a friendship with the butcher. More than a few times, we've nicely asked a butcher to check in the back to see if there is any grass-fed beef that isn't on display. And that request almost always results in a small victory.

In the following pages, we've laid out what to look for when purchasing certain types of ingredients. Our mentality is to do the best you can with what you have. Don't worry that you aren't doing Paleo "correctly" if you aren't buying a certain quality of food. Naturally, you want to source the best food you can afford from what is available to you, but while eating organic foods is optimal, it is not essential to your success.

meat

Includes:
Beef, bison, lamb, goat, pork, venison

Packaging terms to look for:
For ruminants (grazing animals), look for terms like organic (ideally certified organic), no antibiotics or hormones used, non-GMO feed, and grass-fed. Pigs are omnivores, so the labeling on good-quality pork typically says "non-GMO, pasture-raised."

Things to be wary of:
If you don't see the terms listed above and cannot verify the source, it could be feedlot meat. Being raised on a feedlot is not ideal for the health of an animal, and consuming the meat of an unhealthy animal only contributes to the illnesses we humans face today.

Buying guide:
Good: Buying natural, hormone-free meat from a grocery store, focusing on leaner cuts, because the fat is where toxins are stored.

Better: Buying organic grass-fed/pasture-raised meat from a grocery store or health food store, or buying non-organic cuts from a local farmer, where you know the animals live a happy life and are well cared for.

Best: Buying organic grass-fed/pasture-raised meat directly from a local farmer or farmers' market. This ensures that you are buying the meat of a well-fed animal that was cared for daily, lived a happy life, and was raised and butchered humanely. Not to mention that you are supporting local farmers who work hard to provide high-quality food for your community.

poultry and eggs

Includes:
Chicken, turkey, duck, game hens, eggs

Packaging terms to look for:
Organic feed, non-GMO feed, soy-free feed, pasture-raised. Some chicken farmers will even give you an estimate of population density per acre. Fewer than 350 chickens per acre is a sustainable number for a commercial operation that supplements free-ranging chickens with feed. Feed should be non-GMO and non-soy if possible.

Things to be wary of:
Vegetarian-fed chicken (chickens are omnivores, not vegetarians). The terms "cage-free" and "free-range" do not necessarily mean that the chickens lived outdoors. If you want meat or eggs from a chicken that roamed around a farm and lived the way nature intended, be sure to purchase pasture-raised poultry and eggs.

Buying guide:
Good: Buying free-range poultry or eggs from a grocery store.

Better: Buying organic poultry or eggs from a grocery store, or buying non-organic, pasture-raised poultry or eggs from a local farmer.

Best: Buying organic, pasture-raised poultry or eggs supplemented with non-GMO and soy-free feed from a health food store or directly from a local farmer or farmers' market.

seafood

Includes:
All varieties of fish and shellfish

Packaging terms to look for:
Wild-caught, sustainably caught, line-caught. Many stores display fish population sustainability data with their fish, provided by the Marine Stewardship Council (MSC). We advocate options that do not compromise fish populations or utilize improper fishing methods that can harm other marine wildlife.

Things to be wary of:
Avoid farm-raised fish due to the feed offered and the living conditions of the fish. Also give consideration to fish size. The larger the fish, the higher up the food chain it is. This means that it has a longer life span and thus more exposure to marine pollution. Small fish like sardines are an excellent choice because they have very low toxicity.

Buying guide:
Good: Limiting consumption to canned or smoked wild-caught fish if fresh, wild-caught fish is not available for purchase near you.

Better: Buying canned or fresh wild-caught seafood from a grocery store.

Best: Buying sustainably raised or wild-caught fish from your local fishmonger, choosing varieties that are low in mercury. In better stores, fresh fish is delivered daily.

vegetables and fruits

Includes:
Anything that grows above or below ground as a vegetable, fruit, or tuber

Terms to look for:
Organic, pesticide-free, heirloom. If you're shopping in a grocery store, organic produce will have a 5-digit PLU that begins with the number 9. Also look for produce that is in season and locally grown. When buying frozen vegetables, always opt for organic, and read the label to see if the product contains any suspicious ingredients or preservatives.

Things to be wary of:
Some grocery stores will do anything to provide produce year-round, even if it cannot be grown in that area year-round. This means shipping produce from far away (like Argentina or Chile), shipping produce before it's ripe, or coating produce with a heavy layer of wax. Avoid genetically modified (GMO) produce, which has a PLU that begins with the number 8. Try to buy organic produce whenever possible, especially if you're going to eat the skin or outer layer.

Buying guide:
Good: Buying non-organic produce from a grocery store, avoiding the "Dirty Dozen" (opposite).

Better: Buying organic produce from a grocery store, or buying locally grown, non-organic produce from a farmer.

Best: Buying organic, in-season produce from a grocery store, or buying locally grown, organic produce from a farmer or farmers' market. Another option is to join a CSA (community supported agriculture) program, which is a great way to encourage in-season cooking. Local farmers put together boxes of their best in-season crops for you to cook from and deliver them (or make them available for pickup at a central location) on a regular basis.

Better than best: Growing your own produce! Starting a small garden bed is a really fun way to get connected to your food. Gardening is relaxing and very rewarding, not to mention that being able to pick your own lettuce, cucumbers, carrots, or herbs right before eating ensures that you are getting the most nutrients possible from those plants!

Dirty Dozen+

always buy organic

01. apples
02. strawberries
03. grapes
04. celery
05. peaches
06. spinach
07. bell peppers
08. nectarines
09. cucumbers
10. tomatoes
11. snap peas
12. potatoes
13. hot peppers
14. kale/collard greens

Clean 15

okay to buy conventional

01. avocados
02. sweet corn
03. pineapples
04. cabbage
05. sweet peas
06. onions
07. asparagus
08. mangoes
09. papayas
10. kiwi
11. eggplant
12. grapefruit
13. cantaloupe
14. cauliflower
15. sweet potatoes

Source: Environmental Working Group 2014 updated lists

healthy fats and oils

saturated fats

Includes:
Coconut oil, palm shortening, butter, ghee (clarified butter), lard, tallow, schmaltz (chicken fat), duck fat

Things to look for:
Saturated fats are the most stable fats, which means that heat does little damage to their fatty acid profile. Saturated fats are always solid at room temperature.

For coconut oil, organic virgin is your best option.

When purchasing palm shortening, be sure that it comes from a source that does not harm the orangutan habitat. We use Spectrum Organic.

For butter and ghee, organic grass-fed is the best choice. (You can also make your own ghee; our recipe is on pg 286.)

When purchasing animal fats, make sure that they come from pastured animals that were fed a healthy diet. It's always nice to render your own meat-derived fats. We have a great recipe for Rendered Lard on pg 294. You can do the same with tallow, schmaltz, and duck fat—the process is very similar.

oils

Includes:
Extra-virgin olive oil, avocado oil, sesame oil, macadamia nut oil

Things to look for:
Cold-pressed or expeller-pressed, organic, extra-virgin, non-GMO, and unrefined. When purchasing oils, look for dark glass bottles or opaque containers, which protect the fats from oxidation.

Things to be wary of:
Fats are some of the trickiest ingredients for Paleo newbies to get straight. Avoid seed oils like canola oil, grapeseed oil, sunflower seed oil, soybean oil, and safflower oil, as well as peanut oil. These types of oils are typically rancid on the shelves before you even purchase them, and they are easily damaged when heated, which contributes to inflammation in the body. Canola oil is often used in restaurants, so making an effort to eat more home-cooked meals is important. Seed oils are often hidden in commercial salad dressings and other types of products. For this reason, we make our own dressings or purchase the Tessemae's brand, which uses pure, extra-virgin olive oil.

nuts and seeds

Includes:
Almonds, Brazil nuts, cashews, chestnuts, hazelnuts, macadamia nuts, pecans, pine nuts, pistachios, walnuts, chia seeds, flax seed, hemp seeds, poppy seeds, pumpkin seeds, sesame seeds, sunflower seeds

Things to consider:
Organic and raw are your best options. Nuts and seeds contain a high amount of omega-6 fatty acids, which are not heat-stable, so roasted nuts may contain damaged fats, which contribute to inflammation in the body. Soaked and sprouted nuts and seeds are the easiest to digest, but if you can't find soaked and sprouted or dehydrated nuts and seeds at your local store, you can easily soak and dehydrate your own raw nuts and seeds at home. Soaking and dehydrating nuts and seeds eliminates the phytic acid, an antinutrient that inhibits the absorption of minerals from the other foods you are eating.

Buying guide:
Good: Buying non-organic raw nuts and seeds.

Better: Buying organic raw nuts and seeds.

Best: Buying organic, raw, soaked and sprouted nuts and seeds.

herbs, spices, and seasonings

Includes:
Fresh and dried herbs, spices, herb salts, spice blends

Things to look for:
Look for purity here. Herbs and spices not only flavor your food, but also can be a powerful component of healing the body, so be sure that you purchase organic, non-GMO herbs, spices, and spice blends. Salt, which is a mineral, serves to enhance the flavor of your dishes. We always opt for unrefined sea salt, such as pink Himalayan sea salt, which is packed with essential trace minerals and offers many health benefits.

Things to be wary of:
Steer clear of spice blends that have extra ingredients, like anticoagulants. (Also look for anticoagulants such as calcium silicate and sodium aluminosilicate in salt.)

Buying guide:
Better: Buying organic spices and fresh herbs when possible.

Best: Growing your own herbs! There's nothing quite like using fresh-picked herbs for cooking.

unique ingredients used in this book

coconut aminos

What is it?

Coconut aminos is a delicious soy sauce alternative and a staple in a Paleo pantry. Coconut aminos is made from the sap of the coconut tree, which is aged with a sun-dried, mineral-rich sea salt. Coconut aminos can be used in marinades, stir-fries, salad dressings, and dipping sauces. It's a great way to get a traditional flavor for Asian-inspired dishes, and it's our favorite choice for dipping sushi.

Things to be wary of:

Do not confuse this item with liquid aminos. Although Braggs Liquid Aminos is gluten-free, it is soy-based and best avoided on a Paleo diet.

Where to buy it:

We are able to find coconut aminos at several local grocery stores, but if you can't find it near you, Amazon is a great source.

fish sauce

What is it?

Fish sauce is a liquid derived from the process of fermenting fish (typically anchovies) with sea salt. It is used to impart a salty, briny, umami flavor.

Things to look for:

Most fish sauces are made from just fish and salt. We prefer the Red Boat brand, which is high-quality and readily available.

Things to be wary of:

Check the label to see if any unusual ingredients are added.

katsuobushi (bonito flakes)

What is it?

Katsuobushi is the Japanese name for dried and fermented bonito. The fish are smoked, dried, petrified, and then shaved into delicious, delicate flakes. Together with kombu (see below), it is used as the base for dashi, a clear Japanese soup (see pg 284 for our recipe).

Things to look for:

Bags are typically labeled completely in Japanese if you get them at a Japanese food store. You can sometimes find these in health food stores with packaging written in English. Inside the package you will see thin, pink fish flakes.

Things to be wary of:

As with any product, inspect the ingredient list. The ingredients for katsuobushi should say "Dried Bonito." Avoid products that contain additional ingredients.

kombu

What is it?

Kombu is a dried kelp used to season broths and stocks. Unlike the thin sheets of nori used for sushi, Kombu is thick and dark in color. Along with katsuobushi (see above), it forms the basis of dashi.

Things to look for:

Read the packaging for purity of ingredients. The ingredients should just say "Kombu."

Things to be wary of:

Kombu is high in iodine. If you suffer from thyroid conditions, consume dishes flavored with kombu only if you know that your body can tolerate that amount of iodine.

grain-free baking

Like making a good, home-cooked meal, there is something about baking that we seem to hold dear to our hearts as human beings. It brings about a sense of family, love, teaching, and sharing. We can probably all say that we have fond memories of baking a special treat for a holiday or special occasion, and of the recipes that our parents or grandparents taught to us, which we can then pass down to future generations. Just because you are making a lifestyle change does not mean that you have to eliminate those experiences from your life or a family member's. With a few ingredient swaps, you can make delicious desserts to enjoy with family and friends that won't prevent you from living a life of better health. In this section, we'll tell you about our favorite grain-free baking ingredients and how you can use them in your kitchen.

grain-free flours and starches

The two most common grain-free flours are blanched almond flour and coconut flour. Both can create decadent cakes, cupcakes, cookies, and pie crusts, but each works completely differently.

blanched almond flour

Blanched almond flour is made by grinding raw almonds that have had their skins removed into a fine powder. This flour is quite versatile and translates very well as a grain-free alternative to conventional wheat flour. We have even subbed blanched almond flour one-for-one with wheat flour to re-create an old family recipe, and it turned out wonderfully. Almond flour can be used in cakes, breads, cupcakes, cookies, pie crusts, and crumbles.

coconut flour

Coconut flour is made by grinding dehydrated coconut meat into a fine powder. This grain-free flour is versatile, like blanched almond flour, but it can be a bit trickier to work with. Coconut flour is very dense and tends to absorb a lot of moisture, so it's best used in small amounts and blended with a starch (see below) and a good amount of liquid so that your baked goods are enjoyable to eat.

tapioca starch and arrowroot starch

Starches are a huge part of grain-free baking. They completely alter the texture of a baked good before being baked and after. They lighten what is typically a pretty dense batter made from almond flour or coconut flour. They also can create the perfect stretchy consistency for cookie-cutter cookies or pie crusts. Have you ever tried to make a pie crust and had it crumble to pieces when you tried to mold it to your pie pan? Adding some tapioca starch or arrowroot starch will enable you to roll out a beautiful pie crust that will hold its shape for any presentation you like.

Tapioca is the starch extracted from the cassava plant, and arrowroot is the starch extracted from the roots of the arrowroot plant. Tapioca starch and arrowroot starch are interchangeable on a one-for-one basis; which one you use depends on your personal preference or whether you find that you are unable to tolerate one or the other.

natural sweeteners

What would a dessert be without sugar? A savory baked good, that's what. When implementing healthier alternatives in baking, choosing the right kind of sugar is important, but how will it affect your baked goods? We use several types of sweeteners when baking, usually for different tastes.

raw honey and pure maple syrup

Raw honey and pure maple syrup are probably the most commonly used sweeteners in the Paleo world. Raw honey has many health benefits: It contains natural antioxidants, enzymes, and minerals and can even prevent or help ward off seasonal allergies. Pure maple syrup is famous for dressing pancakes and waffles with a warm, gooey sweetness, but it also lends a nice flavor to baked goods. We use these liquid sweeteners interchangeably in baked goods that benefit from the added moisture. If one of our recipes calls for 1/2 cup of pure maple syrup but all you have is honey, go ahead and use the honey! Honey and maple syrup both have their own wonderful, unique flavors, which can be an added benefit to most baked goods without overpowering the overall taste. If you use honey or maple syrup in a cake or cookies, you likely won't taste the honey or maple flavor, just the sweetness. If you are using it to make ice cream, sweeten whipped cream, or make a meringue, however, you may notice the honey or maple flavor in your dessert.

granulated maple sugar

This is our top choice for a granulated cane sugar alternative. Because it is not a liquid, you don't have to worry about granulated maple sugar changing the consistency of your baked goods. With its mild maple flavor, it works well in most baking recipes; you will see it used to make ice cream, cakes, cookies, and pies. The only time we really notice the maple flavor is when it's used in vanilla ice cream, but who doesn't love maple vanilla ice cream?

Depending on the source of your maple sugar, the granules can vary in texture and size. If you have purchased a maple sugar that is fairly coarse, give it a pulse in your food processor to create a finer, more powderlike texture. This will give your baked goods a better texture, because the sugar will dissolve completely into the batter.

coconut sugar

Coconut sugar is derived from the sap of the coconut palm tree. It is a dark, caramel-brown color, similar to brown sugar, and is very coarse. Although coconut sugar can be used in place of granulated maple sugar in most of the recipes in this book, you should be aware that it will change the flavor and color of your baked goods slightly. We prefer to use coconut sugar in small amounts when the color and texture are an added benefit, such as in a streusel topping or a cinnamon-sugar blend for cinnamon rolls.

chocolate

When baking, we always use Enjoy Life chocolate chips because they are allergen-free. Their mini morsels are more of a semi-sweet and their regular morsels are more of a dark chocolate, so you have two options depending on your preference. We use them for just about anything that requires either the addition of chocolate chips or a melted chocolate drizzle or candy coating.

Another good option for baking chocolate is the Eating Evolved brand. We love all of their products. Their chocolate bars and cocoa powder are perfect for baking and are completely allergen-free!

nut milks

Nut milks are handy staples in a grain-free kitchen for baking and other uses. Nut milks are great dairy alternatives that can be poured over grain-free granola or even added to coffee as a creamer. We love using almond milk to make nondairy milkshakes. It can also be added to breads or cake batters to lend a touch of moisture. Most commercial almond milk beverages contain undesirable ingredients, so we try to make nut milks fresh at home. Our recipe for homemade nut milk can be found on pg 300.

coconut milk

We love using coconut milk and coconut cream (described at right) for making desserts. Full-fat coconut milk is a fantastic base for dairy-free ice cream and a great option for adding a touch of moisture to baked goods made from coconut flour. We always use canned coconut milk, because the boxed liquid beverage versions contain many undesirable ingredients. When purchasing canned coconut milk, the only ingredients should be coconut meat, water, and a thickening agent (typically guar gum). We prefer Native Forest brand because it is all organic, uses purified water, and comes in BPA-free cans. If you cannot tolerate guar gum, then we recommend using the Natural Value brand of coconut milk, because it is free of guar gum and also comes in BPA-free containers. Just be sure to purchase the organic version.

coconut cream

Coconut cream is simply the thick cream that separates from the water in a can of coconut milk. This is what you need to make the Whipped Coconut Cream found on pg 398. This nondairy version of heavy whipping cream can be used to frost cupcakes and cakes, make parfaits, pipe decorations on pies, or simply enjoyed over berries.

To extract the cream from the water, place your can of coconut milk in the refrigerator overnight. The cream will rise and separate from the water as it chills. Every once in a while, we get a can that won't separate, so we tend to give the can a gentle shake before choosing to use it for cream. If it seems like the cream is pretty solid already, then we'll refrigerate that can. You can also stick a few extra cans in the fridge for backup.

leavening agents

Baking soda and baking powder are used to make baked goods rise. Baking powder can be used in place of baking soda in most recipes (you just need more of it), but using baking soda in place of baking powder doesn't always work. If a recipe calls for baking powder and you have only baking soda on hand, then you'll need some sort of acid to help activate the baking soda (think science class, where baking soda is added to vinegar in a model of a volcano to make it erupt). With baking powder, that acid is cream of tartar. Most commercial baking powder products contain cornstarch, so it's best to avoid them. We love the Hain brand of baking powder because it uses potato starch instead of cornstarch, but for those who avoid nightshades, we created a simple recipe for baking powder, found on pg 274. This homemade version works really well to help baked goods rise, better than any other baking powder we have tried!

kitchen tools

Most of the dishes in this book can be made using a few select tools. You don't have to have a kitchen that looks like the inside of a Williams-Sonoma store to create delicious meals (though it never hurts!). Here are some of our favorite tools, and some tools that you'll want to have on hand to make our recipes.

Much like the quality of ingredients you use, the quality of your equipment can greatly impact the outcome of your dishes. We're not talking about the difference between a $2 can opener and an $8 can opener, either. Your cooking tools can affect your ability to modulate and control heat as it relates to the food you're cooking, for example. Pots and pans are made from materials of varying quality. A professional-quality, copper-core, stainless-steel sauté pan will distribute and maintain heat much more evenly than a lower-quality aluminum or nonstick pan. Similarly, the quality of your knives, the accuracy of your measuring devices, and the power and reliability of your appliances all play a role in your ability to accurately replicate these recipes. The following tools are the ones we recommend you invest in for a better cooking experience.

a few good knives

When cooking with fresh ingredients, one of the most common steps is to cut them down into manageable pieces. The best choice for most cutting needs is a chef's knife, which typically is 10 inches long and has a gently curved blade. You can do more than half of your cutting with this one knife. Other good blades to have in your collection are a paring knife (short and stiff, good for peeling and small tasks) and a knife with a serrated blade for cutting foods like tomatoes. Our four favorites are shown on the opposite page. Keep your knives sharp; a dull blade can be dangerous, and an easy way to cut yourself! Use wood cutting boards with your good knives; cutting on a hard surface could damage them. Take care to wash knives shortly after using them, dry them immediately, and return them to their knife block or other safe place to preserve their edges.

stainless-steel skillets
(10 inches and 12 inches)

Unlike cast iron (see below), stainless-steel skillets do not retain any nonstick properties from use to use. They are perfect for cooking food evenly over a gas flame. If you have an electric range, you can still use high-quality pans (such as those made by All-Clad), though you may need to adjust your cooking temperatures, as electric ranges behave differently. We like the full-stainless skillets that also have stainless handles because they can go from the stovetop to the oven just like cast iron, which is great for making frittatas, potatoes, and lamb chops. They're also easy to clean! To keep food from sticking, use a liberal amount of saturated fat, and cook things like eggs low and slow until they release freely from the skillet.

a heavy cast-iron skillet

For about $30, you can buy a Lodge cast-iron skillet that will literally last forever. Cast-iron skillets can be transferred from the stovetop to the oven, a method we use in a few recipes. The benefit is the ability to sear the meat you're cooking, then move the pan to the oven to gently cook the meat the rest of the way through. Many people are reluctant to use cast iron because they don't know how to season it properly. To season a cast-iron pan, very gently cook bacon in it for the first three or four uses. After the bacon has cooked, pour off the fat (and save it for cooking). Give the pan a brief rinse with hot water, wipe it out, and use a paper towel to regrease the pan with some coconut oil. That's it! This process will build up a nice seasoning on the pan without creating extra work. Besides, you'll get to enjoy some bacon! To keep the seasoning on the pan, never use soap or any harsh cleaner; just rinse it with hot water and a sponge or stiff brush, wipe it with a towel, and then reapply some coconut oil.

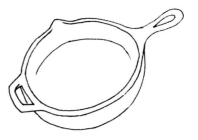

stainless-steel saucepans

(½ quart, 2 quart, and 3 quart)

These three sizes are all you'll ever need. We love our little 1/2-quart saucepan; it's just the right size for melting coconut oil, grass-fed butter, and lard. The 2- and 3-quart saucepans are perfect for bringing together sauces, like our Pizza Sauce (pg 256), and for steaming small quantities of vegetables.

heavy dutch oven or tagine

A big, heavy pot with a big, heavy lid is great for making traditional slow-cooked dishes. Being able to put the pot over medium-high heat allows you to sear the meat in the vessel and then continue cooking without losing any flavor. This is a clear advantage over a slow cooker, with which you must sear the meat or vegetables in a separate skillet before adding them to the slow cooker.

large stockpot

Perfect for simmering stocks and broths and for making big batches of soup, a large stockpot is a necessity in any well-stocked kitchen. We prefer a stainless-steel stockpot.

slow cooker

A slow cooker isn't just for people who are short on time. A slow cooker is great for making bone broth or breaking down tough cuts of meat into tender mouthfuls. There are many ways to utilize this inexpensive and versatile tool. Anytime we call for a tagine or Dutch oven (see above), you can almost surely use a slow cooker instead. If you do use a slow cooker, expect cook times to be 25 percent longer, in general.

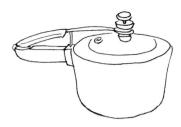

pressure cooker

Don't be afraid to use a pressure cooker. You've surely heard a horror story or two about pressure cookers blowing up, but we've never had an experience like that. When used properly, a pressure cooker is quite safe and effective at reducing cooking times. Our favorite way to use ours is to make stock in an hour, as described on pg 278. Other methods have you simmering the stock for twelve to twenty-four hours, but if you need stock quickly, a pressure cooker is your best bet. To streamline things, we often make the stock in the pressure cooker, strain out the bones, and then add soup ingredients directly to the pot and simmer it without the lid.

high-speed blender

We rely heavily on our high-speed blender. The high power output of this tool can pulverize nuts into nut butters and whip air into puréed vegetables (like our Sweet Potato Puree on pg 196 and Celery Root Puree on pg 200). You can also make smoothies, ice creams, and soups. There are good choices on the market from brands like Blendtec, Ninja, and Vitamix. Whichever brand you choose, you really can't go wrong. If a high-speed blender isn't in your budget, don't fret! Most of the functionality can be replicated with a food processor or regular blender.

electric hand mixer

For small mixing jobs, an electric hand mixer is a great tool to have in your kitchen. We use ours to whip egg whites, bring together doughs and batters for cookies and cakes, and whip coconut milk or butter into silky-smooth frostings. One great feature of this simple little machine is that you can detach the beaters and throw them in the dishwasher for easy cleanup.

stand mixer

When a hand mixer won't cut it, you'll want a stand mixer. We have a classic (some would say "iconic") KitchenAid stand mixer. We use it primarily for baking endeavors, like whipping up buttercream frostings, mixing batters and doughs, and bringing egg whites to stiff peaks. As an added bonus, some stand mixers have an interface for attachments. We've used ours to attach a meat grinder for making sausage. You can also buy a pasta roller, which is great for making our pasta on pg 328.

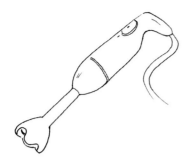

immersion blender

An immersion blender or "stick blender" has many uses, but our two favorites are making Homemade Mayonnaise (pg 244) and puréeing soups. After using a stick blender for making mayonnaise, there's no turning back to any other method. The control and precision offered by an immersion blender makes emulsifying oils consistent and easy. We also love that the blender end is dishwasher-safe!

measuring tools

Dry measuring cups, liquid measuring cups, and measuring spoons are all necessities for accurately replicating recipes. A digital kitchen scale, which is used to measure ingredients by weight, is also handy, especially for baking, where precision is important. In some of the baking recipes in this book, we've included gram weights in addition to volume (cup) measurements for dry ingredients because using gram weights is the more accurate way to replicate the exact measurements. (For example, a packed cup of almond flour will weigh more than a loosely filled cup.) Since we measure the weight of dry ingredients individually by recipe and first by volume, 1 cup of almond flour in one of our recipes might weigh slightly more or less than 1 cup of almond flour in another of our recipes.

mixing bowls

We have several sets of mixing bowls, and each set plays a different role. We use our stainless-steel bowls for making double boilers, placed over a simmering pan of water on the stovetop, to gently melt chocolate or thicken Lemon Curd (pg 376). A ten-piece set of nested glass mixing bowls provides a wide variety of sizes for *mise en place* cooking (where you have everything prepared and set out before you begin to cook). We use plastic bowls with spouts for making batters and sauces; however, we generally prefer glass or stainless steel. Naturally, it's not necessary to have more than one set, but selecting a set based on your particular cooking preferences ensures that you will use them often.

cooking techniques

The goal of this book is to help you learn basic cooking techniques that you can apply broadly in the kitchen, with or without a recipe to follow. Most of the time, the two of us head into the kitchen, check out which ingredients we have, and just start making dinner. Do we have a game plan? Sure. But most times, we don't even think about following a recipe. We rely on our understanding of fundamental cooking techniques and pairing flavor profiles to bring together great meals with ease.

That's the beauty of truly learning to cook. With some practice, you will sharpen your instincts in the kitchen, and you'll be able to work without a recipe. You'll learn how to measure salt by pinching it with your fingers, or how to determine the internal temperature of a steak by its firmness. The following pages outline the basic techniques that we use in many of our recipes.

pan-searing

Putting a good sear on meat helps lock in moisture and flavor. It also gives the meat a slight crust, which improves the texture, too! The idea here is to start with a skillet over medium to medium-high heat. Add some fat, at least enough to coat the bottom of the pan completely. Watch the pan closely. When the fat is hot, add the meat and sear it until it is nicely browned, which usually takes 2 to 3 minutes per side. One of the tricks is to manage the temperature of the pan and the amount of fat in the pan. If the temperature is too hot, the fat will cook off and the meat could burn. If the temperature is too low, the meat will not sear properly. Recipes that use this technique include Lamb Chops with Maple Balsamic Glaze (pg 82), Nightshade-Free Breakfast Sausage (pg 88), and Skillet Chicken Thighs (pg 136).

sautéing

To sauté means to fry quickly in a little bit of oil or fat. *Sauté* is the French word for stir-fry. For this method of cooking, you want to use a skillet and smaller sliced or chopped vegetables or meat. Saturated fat is ideal for sautéing, since you generally want to use a higher heat to sauté food. The goal is to sear the vegetables or meat in a short time, allowing for the preservation of textures, flavors, and moisture in the food. It is similar to pan-searing, but when sautéing you are cooking the food to the desired doneness. And, as with pan-searing, when sautéing meat you can use the cooked bits on the bottom of the skillet as the base of flavor for making a sauce to go over your dish. Recipes that use this technique include Breakfast Beef Hash (pg 66), Basic Cauliflower Rice (pg 188), and Ethiopian Cabbage (pg 204).

braising

A simple yet flavorful way of cooking, braising always screams comfort food to us. To braise simply means to cook meat and vegetables slowly in a liquid. Braising is a combination of pan-searing and slow cooking, and typically you use a tagine or Dutch oven. You start by searing your meat on the stovetop, preferably in a saturated fat, seasoned with sea salt. Once the meat has a good sear on it, you remove it from the pot. If you like, you can add a mirepoix (usually a combination of chopped onion, celery, and carrots) for flavor, sautéing these vegetables in the same pot over medium heat and scraping up the brown bits. Once the vegetables are caramelized, you remove them from the pot and then deglaze the pot with your choice of liquid: stock, wine, or a combination of both. The key is not to add so much liquid that the meat is submerged. This would be boiling the meat, not braising it. Then you add the meat back to the pot with the braising liquid, cover, and allow it to cook for several hours, either on the stovetop or in the oven on a lower heat setting. To complete the dish, you add the caramelized vegetables toward the end of the cooking time, typically 45 minutes to 1 hour before the dish is done. Recipes that use this technique include Braised Lamb Shanks (pg 64) and Braised Brussels Sprouts (pg 192).

slow cooking

Slow cooking is best for roasts and tough cuts of meat. Applying a low temperature over a long period breaks down the meat, allowing it to become tender and juicy. Although the concept of slow cooking makes it seem as though you need to allow a whole day to tend to the food, this method is particularly helpful for people who don't have much time to cook. You just need a roast of your choice, some stock or tomato-based liquid, and lots of vegetables, and you allow them to cook unattended in the slow cooker for 8 to 10 hours. The meal will cook safely on your countertop without needing your attention, so you can go about your day, and all that you'll need to do to get ready for dinner is set the table. Recipes that use this technique include Beef Daube (pg 60) and Moroccan Short Ribs (pg 86).

steaming

If you're new to cooking, steaming is an easy technique used to gently cook vegetables (or dumplings) by bathing them in a cloud of steam. There are a few different types of steamers, but we almost always use a metal steamer basket. Some sets of pots and pans have a dedicated steamer pot (with holes) that fits a matching pot (without holes), which is nice for big jobs like a batch of dumplings or large vegetables such as artichokes. For smaller jobs like cauliflower florets, you can use a stainless-steel steamer basket that fits most saucepans. Add at least 1 inch of water to the bottom pot, cover, and heat over medium-high heat until it begins to steam. Add the desired ingredients and reduce the heat slightly. One thing to be aware of is monitoring the amount of water as compared to cook time. Foods like artichokes take a very long time, and you may need to add more water.

stock making

Homemade stock is the base of many great, traditional meals. Making a flavorful stock is very easy, and despite the rising popularity of bone broth in mainstream products, we guarantee that you'll never get better flavor than when you make it yourself. Many people use *broth* and *stock* interchangeably, but there is a minor difference: broth is made from meat, and stock is made from bones. It is because of this slight difference that "bone broth" is a commonly used misnomer.

We love having the option to use our pressure cooker to make stock, because we often have trouble planning twelve to twenty-four hours ahead for recipes. Our favorite chicken stock is so easy to make: six chicken backs, water to cover them, and a splash of apple cider vinegar to help extract the beneficial minerals from the bones. Lock the lid, raise the heat, and, when the pressure cooker starts to hiss, lower the heat to medium and set a timer for one hour. Adjust the temperature up or down depending on how much the pot is hissing. You want a steady, gentle to moderate hiss.

A more traditional way to make stock, and our favorite way, is to fill a stockpot with roasted animal bones, organic carrots, celery, onion, smashed garlic, peppercorns, and sea salt. Cover with water, bring to a boil, and then allow to simmer on low heat, uncovered, for fifteen hours. Tending to the stock every so often is important so you know that it isn't burning. There's nothing worse than the flavor of burnt vegetables in nutrient-dense stock. This possibility is the reason we tend to avoid using a slow cooker for making stock with vegetables; the heat is easier to regulate when the stock is simmered on the stovetop. (If you use a slow cooker to make your stock, we recommend using just bones and water.) When the stock has finished cooking, remove the bones and strain the stock. Allow the stock to cool, and remove the layer of fat that rises to the surface before drinking the stock or using it in soups or stews. You can find our recipes for Chicken Stock and Beef Stock on pg 278.

making a reduction

Because wheat flour is off the menu for Paleo cooking, you may wonder how to create a thick, creamy sauce or gravy. Although you may be tempted to add a thickening agent like tapioca starch or arrowroot starch, doing so is not ideal, because those agents tend to make a sauce gummy. The best option for flavor and texture is to reduce the liquid you are cooking over very low heat until it's thick and creamy or, in the case of a sweet-flavored reduction, more like a syrup. This process takes time, but the end result is worth it! For best results, you want to make your sauce in a shallow pan, where it can spread out in a thinner layer and thus cook down and reduce more quickly. Stirring or whisking often while reducing a sauce is important, especially in a shallow skillet, to keep it from burning. If you're making a gravy, adding puréed cooked onion or even white potato is a fantastic option for thickening that also enhances the flavor. Recipes that use this technique include our Stuffed Chicken Thighs (pg 140), Lobster Fettuccine Alfredo (pg 160), and Caramelized Maple Balsamic (pg 234).

grilling

Much like pan-searing, cooking meat on a grill or in a grill pan is all about heat management. In fact, most cooking comes down to heat management. There is definitely a difference between using a grill pan, a gas grill, and a charcoal grill. A grill pan is simply a pan with raised ribs that can be used on the stovetop in lieu of a grill. While it can deliver the signature look of grilled food, it does not impart the flavors of true grilled food. A gas grill is great for the sake of convenience, wherein the fire is fueled with propane or natural gas. A gas grill can easily and quickly modulate and redistribute heat, making it easy to use for cooking. Charcoal and wood-fired grills are the tools of choice for the purists out there. The strong allure of these grills is their ability to impart flavors of wood smoke (or hints of smoky charcoal) into the food, but the drawback is that they are difficult to control for temperature and also require frequent cleaning.

No matter which grilling tool you're using, you need to know how to deliver a sear, how to cook food over direct heat, and how to cook food slowly with indirect heat. With red meat like steak, you want to deliver a good sear over higher heat and then finish over gentle heat to keep the moisture inside the meat while lightly cooking it to medium or medium-rare doneness. If you're working with a grill pan, the same principles apply. Outdoor grilling is a great way to deliver big flavor and keep your kitchen clean. In the summer, it also keeps your kitchen cool! Recipes that use this technique include Grilled Sirloin Skewers (pg 78), Pork Chops with Apple Chutney (pg 94), and Honey Sesame Wings (pg 124).

warm smoking

While smoking is not a heavily utilized technique in this book, it's one that can really take your cooking to the next level. There are two main types of smoking: cold smoking and warm smoking. The recipes in this book rely on warm smoking, which delivers not only smoke but also gentle heat. Cold smoking delivers only a smoke flavor. Cold smoking is best for foods like bacon and cheese, as it prevents the food from cooking. Warm smoking is ideal for making a slow-cooked pork shoulder with a thick, smoky crust. Smoking could encompass a cookbook unto itself, and we don't profess to know everything there is to know about smoking. What we do know is that a smoky flavor can really enhance certain dishes. Recipes that use this technique include our Smoked Ribs (pg 106), Smoked Flounder Hand Rolls (pg 174), and Cured Bacon (pg 280). If you do not have a smoker, each of these recipes includes cooking and flavoring alternatives.

pickling, fermenting, and curing

These traditional methods of food preservation have their roots in nontropical cultures, where food became scarce during the colder months. Through the use of salt, vinegar, and sugar, pickling, fermenting, and curing help preserve foods in a variety of ways by creating hostile environments for bad bacteria. You'll find a few recipes in this book that use these techniques, like our Cured Bacon (pg 280), Cured Salmon (pg 282), and even Pickled Burdock Root (pg 290).

meat

beef daube

Serves: **4–6**   Prep time: **30 minutes**   Cook time: **3 hours**

• Nut-free   • Egg-free

66 Beef Daube is a classic French stew of braised beef, red wine, and vegetables. The Beef Daube that you see today is often served over egg noodles. We serve our version of this fragrant and rich dish over cauliflower rice. This crowd-pleasing recipe is the perfect comfort food for a cool fall evening or a cold winter night. 99

2 Tbsp unsalted grass-fed butter

10 cloves garlic, smashed with the side of a knife

2 lbs beef stew meat, cut into 1-inch chunks

Sea salt

1 cup red wine

1 cup chopped Vidalia onion

3 large carrots, peeled and chopped

4 stalks celery, chopped

1 Tbsp tomato paste

1 (14 1/2-oz) can diced tomatoes

1/2 cup Beef Stock (pg 278)

10 grinds black pepper

1/2 tsp dried rosemary

1/2 tsp dried thyme

Serve with Basic Cauliflower Rice (pg 188)

Preheat the oven to 300°F.

Melt the butter in a large ovenproof soup pot over medium heat. Add the garlic and sauté until fragrant. Remove the garlic from the pot and set aside. Add the beef to the pot in small batches and sear on all sides, seasoning with salt.

Remove the beef from the pot and set aside. Add the red wine, scraping up any brown bits on the bottom of the pot. Stir in the onion, carrots, and celery. Once the vegetables soften slightly, about 5 minutes, add the tomato paste and diced tomatoes and stir to combine all of the ingredients. Return the beef and garlic to the pot and stir to combine.

Pour in the stock and season with salt and 10 grinds of pepper. Add the rosemary and thyme and stir to combine the ingredients.

Bring the stew to a boil, then turn off the burner, cover with a lid, and place in the oven for 2–2 1/2 hours, until the beef is tender.

Transfer the stew from the oven to the stovetop. Remove the lid and simmer over medium-low heat until the liquid has reduced by 1 inch, stirring often to prevent any bits on the bottom from burning. Serve immediately, or lower the heat to keep the stew warm until ready to serve.

Cook's Note:

To make this recipe dairy-free, use ghee or lard instead of butter.

braised beef heart

Serves: **4**   Prep time: **25 minutes**   Cook time: **2 hours**

· Nut-free   · Egg-free

1 beef heart (1 1/2 pounds; see Notes)

1/2 tsp sea salt

1 Tbsp coconut oil

1 Tbsp unsalted grass-fed butter

1 Vidalia onion, chopped

2 large cloves garlic, smashed with the side of a knife and chopped

Ground black pepper

4 Roma tomatoes, seeded and chopped

3 medium carrots, peeled and chopped

1 tsp dried oregano

1 tsp dried basil

1 bay leaf

1 1/2 cups strained tomatoes

1/2 lb fingerling potatoes, sliced in half

Rinse the beef heart under cold water and pat dry with a paper towel. Slice it into 1-inch cubes and sprinkle with the salt.

Heat a 7-quart enameled Dutch oven over medium-high heat. Melt the coconut oil in the pot and sear the beef heart in batches until browned on all sides, about 10 minutes total, adjusting the heat as needed if the oil starts to get too hot. Remove the browned beef heart from the pot and set aside.

Reduce the heat to medium-low. Add the butter, onion, and garlic and sauté until fragrant, seasoning with a pinch each of salt and pepper. Once the onion is translucent, add the tomatoes and carrots. Season with the oregano, basil, and bay leaf.

Cook the tomatoes with the onions for about 2 minutes, then return the beef heart to the pot. Pour the strained tomatoes over the beef heart. Reduce the heat to low and simmer for 1 hour, then add the potatoes to the pot and continue cooking. The stew is ready to serve when the beef heart and potatoes are tender, about 2 hours total.

Cook's Notes:

If you do not enjoy beef heart, you can substitute beef stew meat.

To make this recipe dairy-free, use ghee or lard instead of butter.

braised lamb shanks

Serves: **4**   Prep time: **30 minutes**   Cook time: **2 1/2 hours**

· Nut-free   · Egg-free

4 lamb shanks

1 Tbsp unsalted grass-fed butter

1 Vidalia onion, sliced

Sea salt

5 cloves garlic, smashed with the side of a knife

5 stalks celery, with greens

1 sprig fresh rosemary, chopped

1/4 cup balsamic vinegar

1/4 cup coconut aminos

1 cup Beef Stock (pg 278)

Ground black pepper

1 (6-oz) can tomato paste

1 Tbsp Rendered Lard (pg 294)

Remove the lamb shanks from the fridge and allow them to come to room temperature. Rinse under cold water and pat dry with a paper towel.

Melt the butter in a large cast-iron soup pot over medium heat. Add the onion and sauté, adding a pinch of salt to season as well as to cause the onion to release some liquid. After a minute or so, add the garlic to the pot and continue to sauté. After another minute, add the celery and rosemary and continue to sauté until the vegetables have softened, about 5–10 minutes.

Whisk together the balsamic vinegar and coconut aminos, pour over the vegetables in the pot, and stir to combine. Reduce the heat to medium-low and cook the vegetables in the liquid for about 3–5 minutes. Add the stock and stir to combine. Season with a pinch each of salt and pepper. Add the tomato paste to the pot and stir to combine. Cook for about 1 minute, then remove from the heat.

Season the lamb shanks with salt and heat the lard in a cast-iron skillet over high heat. Sear the lamb shanks until browned on all sides, about 5 minutes total. Transfer the lamb shanks to the pot with the vegetables, turning the lamb shanks to coat them with the braising liquid. Bring to a boil, then reduce the heat to a simmer.

Cover and cook for about 2 1/2 hours, checking and rotating the lamb shanks every so often. They are done when the meat is tender and falling off the bone.

Cook's Notes:

To make this recipe dairy-free, use ghee or lard instead of butter.

breakfast beef hash

Serves: **4–6**   Prep time: **25 minutes**   Cook time: **35 minutes**

· Dairy-free   · Nut-free   · Egg-free

Home Fries (pg 206)

1 tsp duck fat or coconut oil

1 lb 85/15 grass-fed ground beef

Sea salt

1/2 Vidalia onion, chopped

1/2 fennel bulb, chopped

2 medium carrots, peeled and chopped

3 stalks celery, chopped

Ground black pepper

Prepare the Home Fries. While they are in the oven, make the beef hash.

In a large cast-iron skillet over medium heat, melt the duck fat. Add the ground beef, season with a pinch of salt, and cook until browned, about 5–10 minutes. Remove the ground beef from the skillet with a slotted spoon and set aside in a small mixing bowl.

If the ground beef released a lot of liquid, allow the liquid to cook off a bit before adding the vegetables. Add the onion to the skillet and sauté over medium heat until it starts to soften, about 2 minutes. Add the fennel, carrots, and celery and season with salt and pepper. Continue to cook over medium to medium-low heat until the vegetables are tender and browned, about 10 minutes.

Return the ground beef to the skillet and stir to combine with the sautéed vegetables. Reduce the heat to a simmer to keep the hash warm until the potatoes have finished roasting.

Remove the Home Fries from the oven, top with the ground beef and vegetable mixture, and serve.

breakfast casserole

Serves: **8**   Prep time: **30 minutes**   Cook time: **40 minutes**

• Dairy-free   • Nut-free

1/2 batch Nightshade-Free Breakfast Sausage (pg 88; see Note)

5 strips bacon

1 sweet potato, peeled and shredded

Sea salt and ground black pepper

1/2 tsp dried oregano

1 Tbsp coconut oil, for greasing the dish

1 Tbsp ghee, store-bought or homemade (pg 286)

1/2 Vidalia onion, chopped

1 medium green bell pepper, chopped

4 Tbsp sliced scallions (2 scallions), divided

8 large eggs

1 cup full-fat coconut milk

Prepare the sausage.

Fry the bacon in a large cast-iron skillet over medium-low heat until slightly crispy, about 8 minutes. Transfer the bacon to paper towels to drain. Pour most of the excess bacon fat from the skillet into a small glass mixing bowl and reserve for later use.

Add the sweet potato to the skillet and season with a pinch of salt, several grinds of pepper, and the oregano. Sauté the sweet potato over medium heat until softened and slightly browned, adding more bacon fat as needed during cooking to prevent it from sticking.

Scoop the browned sweet potato into a large mixing bowl and allow to cool. Chop the sausage patties into bite-sized pieces and add to the sweet potato. Chop the bacon into small bits, reserve 1–2 Tbsp for garnish, and add the remainder to the bowl with the sweet potato.

Preheat the oven to 375°F. Grease a 10-inch round casserole dish with the coconut oil.

Warm the ghee in a clean skillet over medium heat. Add the onion and bell pepper and season with salt and pepper. Sauté until the onion is translucent, about 10 minutes. Add the onion and bell pepper to the bowl with the sweet potato mixture and allow to cool. Add 3 Tbsp of the scallions to the bowl, reserving 1 Tbsp for garnish. Pour the mixture into a greased casserole dish.

In a small mixing bowl, whisk together the eggs and coconut milk. Add a pinch of salt and 5 grinds of pepper. Pour the egg mixture over the vegetable and meat mixture and stir lightly to evenly combine. Bake, uncovered, for 35–40 minutes, until the eggs are firm.

Cook's Note:

As a shortcut, instead of forming the sausage mixture into patties, you can season the ground pork with the spices and then just brown the meat before adding it to this dish.

burgers with pork belly, roasted red peppers, and spicy aioli

Serves: **4**   Prep time: **25 minutes, plus 12–24 hours to marinate**   Cook time: **45 minutes**

• Dairy-free

 " We love burgers with big flavors (and buns, to be honest), so if that's your kind of thing, then you'll like this recipe! If you'd rather skip the lengthy process of making the components, we've outlined some handy shortcuts below. And If you'd rather get right to the good part (eating!), swap out the pork belly for cooked bacon and the homemade Spicy Aioli for our favorite store-bought replacement, Sir Kensington's Chipotle Mayonnaise. "

PORK BELLY

1/2 lb pork belly

2 Tbsp Sweet Pork Rub (pg 272)

BUNS

Grain-Free Sandwich Bread dough (pg 324)

SPICY AIOLI

1/4 cup Homemade Mayonnaise (pg 244)

1 Tbsp chipotle powder

BURGERS

1 1/2 lbs grass-fed ground beef

Sea salt and ground black pepper

TOPPINGS

1 red bell pepper, sliced into wide strips and tossed with cooking fat or oil of choice

4 leaves romaine lettuce (1 per burger)

1 cup arugula (1/4 cup per burger)

Around 12–24 hours before making the burgers, prepare the pork belly. Score the pork belly in a diamond pattern with a sharp knife and rub the Sweet Pork Rub into it. Wrap tightly with plastic wrap and refrigerate for 12–24 hours.

Before cooking the burgers, remove the pork belly from the fridge and allow it to come to room temperature. Meanwhile, make the buns.

Preheat the oven to 350°F. Line a baking sheet with parchment paper and place English muffin rings on top. Make the bread dough, completing the first three steps on pg 324. Pour the dough into the rings, filling them almost completely but leaving a little room for them to rise. Bake for 40 minutes, until a toothpick inserted comes out clean.

While the buns are baking, cook the pork belly: Slice it into 1/2-inch-thick burger-sized slabs and place them in a cold frying pan. Slowly bring up the heat to medium and fry the slabs of belly on both sides until GBD (Golden Brown and Delicious; that's a technical term).

Make the Spicy Aioli by following the Homemade Mayonnaise recipe on pg 244 and adding the chipotle powder. Set aside.

Gently form the beef into 1-inch-thick patties; they should be just firm enough to hold together. Make the patties thinner at the center, as they will pull inward as they cook. Sprinkle with salt and pepper.

Heat your grill to medium. When it reaches 400°F, gently place the burgers on the grill, along with the strips of red bell pepper. After about 4 minutes, flip the burgers and cook for an additional 3 minutes for medium-well. The internal color is a matter of preference, so adjust the cook times accordingly. The roasted red pepper is done when it is soft and lightly blistered.

To assemble the burgers, start with a bottom bun, add a romaine leaf, then a burger, then the toppings (spicy aioli, roasted red pepper, pork belly, and arugula), and finally the top bun.

carne asada with pico de gallo

Serves: **4**   Prep time: **20 minutes, plus 2 hours to marinate**   Cook time: **8–10 minutes**

· Dairy-free   · Nut-free   · Egg-free

MARINADE

2 cloves garlic, minced

1 jalapeño, seeded and minced (see Note)

1 tsp ground cumin

10 sprigs fresh cilantro

Juice of 2 limes (1/4 cup)

Juice of 1/2 orange

6 grinds black pepper

2 pinches of sea salt

1 tsp granulated maple sugar (optional)

1 1/2 lbs flank steak

Pico de Gallo (pg 254), for garnish

Sliced avocado, for garnish (optional)

In a large baking dish or zip-top plastic bag, mix together all of the ingredients for the marinade. Add the flank steak, turn to evenly coat the steak in the marinade, and place in the refrigerator to marinate for 2 hours.

While the steak is marinating, make the Pico de Gallo.

After 2 hours, remove the steak from the refrigerator and allow it to come to room temperature. Meanwhile, preheat a grill to medium-high heat. Grill the steak for about 4–5 minutes per side for medium-rare doneness, or until the desired internal temperature is reached.

Allow the steak to rest for 5 minutes after cooking, then thinly slice it against the grain. Serve with some Pico de Gallo and garnish with avocado slices, if desired.

Cook's Note:

The seeds of the jalapeño contribute piquancy. If you prefer a spicier dish, leave some of the seeds in.

dry-rubbed spareribs

Serves: **2**   Prep time: **30 minutes**   Cook time: **1 hour to smoke or 15–20 minutes to grill**

· Dairy-free   · Nut-free   · Egg-free

 66 This is one of my favorite ways to prepare ribs because it's quick, yet still yields tender, fall-off-the-bone meat. Frankly, ribs are unacceptable any other way. If the meat doesn't fall off the bone, you've done something wrong. This spice blend works well on other cuts of pork, too, so don't hesitate to change things up. If you want to take this recipe to the next level, serve it with our Smoky Barbecue Sauce (pg 262). 99

1 (2-lb) rack pork spareribs

SPICE RUB

2 Tbsp adobo seasoning, store-bought or homemade (pg 272; see Notes)

1 Tbsp sea salt

1 tsp ground turmeric

1 tsp tandoori seasoning, store-bought or homemade (pg 273; see Notes)

1 tsp onion powder

1 tsp paprika

1 tsp dried oregano

1/2 tsp garlic powder

Fill a large pot of water two-thirds full and bring it to a boil. Peel back and remove any silver skin from the underside of the ribs. Place the ribs in the boiling water and parboil for 30 minutes. Remove the ribs from the water and set on a rimmed baking sheet or drying rack to cool.

While the ribs are cooling, combine all of the ingredients for the spice rub in a small mixing bowl. Sprinkle the ribs liberally with the spice rub, covering all sides.

If you have a smoker, smoke the ribs on low (200–220°F) for 1 hour to build a nice smoky flavor. If you don't have a smoker, you can give the ribs some character by grilling them. To use this alternate method, preheat a grill (or grill pan) to medium-low. Place the ribs on the grill and lightly sear for 15–20 minutes, moving them around to ensure that they cook evenly. Serve with barbecue sauce, if desired.

Cook's Notes:

If you don't have adobo seasoning or tandoori seasoning, you can make them yourself using the recipes on pages 272 and 273. Typically they can be found in grocery stores among the other spices and spice blends.

If you have a smoker and would like to build even more flavor, set aside about 4-5 hours for this recipe. Smoke the ribs on low (200-220°F) for 3 hours to start, then wrap them tightly in foil along with a cup of your favorite pure apple juice and smoke over medium heat (250°F) for an additional 1-2 hours.

empanadas

Serves: **4–6**   Prep time: **1 hour**   Cook time: **20 minutes**

• Dairy-free

 "Empanadas are one of the most popular street foods in the Dominican Republic; I ate many of them during my time teaching English there. With no short supply of empanada vendors, my roommates and I quickly found our favorite spot on the far side of Avenido Libertad. The size and filling of these empanadas are inspired by Argentinian-style empanadas. Empanadas in the Dominican Republic are a bit simpler, but I love the bites of sweet currants mixed in with the perfectly spiced beef filling."

FILLING

1 Tbsp duck fat

1/2 medium yellow onion, diced

4 cloves garlic, minced

1 lb ground beef

1 tsp ground cumin

1 tsp dried oregano

1 tsp chili powder

1/2 tsp paprika

1/4 tsp ground cinnamon

1/2 tsp sea salt

1/2 tsp black pepper

1/4 cup dried currants

1 Tbsp plus 1 tsp tomato paste

2 tsp filtered water

Wrapper Dough (pg 336)

Prepare the filling: In a medium-sized skillet, warm the duck fat over medium heat. Add the onion and garlic and sauté until translucent, about 5 minutes. Add the ground beef and spices and continue to cook, breaking up the beef into very small pieces. Once the beef is no longer pink, add the currants, tomato paste, and water. Reduce the heat to medium-low and cook for 10 minutes, then remove from the heat.

Meanwhile, prepare the dough and form it into a ball. Cut two equal-sized sheets of parchment paper to roll out the dough and dust one piece with a little tapioca starch. Place the ball of dough on the dusted parchment. Flatten it gently with your hand, dust it with a little tapioca starch, and place the second sheet of parchment on top. Roll out the dough between the sheets of parchment, gently working your way out from the center of the dough to the edges, until the dough is uniformly 1/8 inch thick. Use a large mason jar lid (about 4 inches in diameter) to cut out circles of dough. Remove the scraps of dough around the circles and set aside to make additional circles after the first set is filled with meat.

Preheat the oven to 350°F. While the oven is heating, form the empanadas: Place about 1 Tbsp of the filling on one-third of a dough circle, fold over the top, crimp the edges with your fingers or a fork, and place on a parchment-lined baking sheet. Repeat this process with the remaining dough and filling. Bake for 20 minutes, until golden brown.

Cook's Note:

If you can't eat nuts, you can use Nut-Free Pasta Dough (pg 328) instead of Wrapper Dough.

grilled sirloin skewers

Serves: **2–4**   Prep time: **15 minutes, plus 2 hours to marinate**   Cook time: **16–20 minutes**

· Dairy-free   · Nut-free   · Egg-free

1 lb sirloin steak, cubed

MARINADE

1/4 cup plus 1 Tbsp fresh lemon juice

1/4 cup extra-virgin olive oil

2 cloves garlic, pressed

1/2 tsp sea salt

10 grinds black pepper

1/4 tsp red pepper flakes

Handful of fresh parsley leaves, chopped

1 red bell pepper

1/2 green bell pepper

1/2 yellow onion

Place the steak in a medium-sized mixing bowl. In a small mixing bowl, whisk together the lemon juice, olive oil, garlic, salt, black pepper, and red pepper flakes. Add the parsley and whisk again to combine. Pour the marinade over the steak, making sure that the marinade covers all of the steak. Cover the bowl and place in the refrigerator to marinate for 2 hours.

After 2 hours, remove the steak from the fridge and allow it to come to room temperature. Meanwhile, prepare the vegetables for the skewers. Cut the bell peppers and onion into chunks similar in size to the cubes of steak.

Alternate the steak and vegetables on the skewers and pour the remaining marinade over the skewers.

Preheat a grill to medium-high heat. Grill the skewers for 4–5 minutes on each of the four sides for medium doneness. Rotate the skewers periodically to encourage even cooking.

Cook's Note:

If you're using wooden skewers, be sure to soak them in water for at least 1 hour prior to grilling to prevent them from catching on fire.

lamb barbacoa tacos

Serves: **6–8**   Prep time: **30 minutes**   Cook time: **4 hours**

· Dairy-free   · Nut-free

"Barbacoa is originally from the Caribbean and Central America, but today there are many varieties of barbacoa dishes. As the dish gained popularity in the American South (particularly Texas), 'barbacoa' became 'barbecue.' Barbacoa gained popularity in many parts of the United States when the restaurant chain Chipotle introduced it as part of its menu. It's easy to see why barbacoa became popular, as it is packed with great flavor and is relatively easy to make. This version with lamb is Mexican, though other regional variations of the dish can be made with beef and pork."

SPICE MIX

1 Tbsp kosher salt

2 tsp paprika

1 tsp ground cumin

1 tsp dried oregano

1/4 tsp chipotle powder

1 cup filtered water

2 lbs boneless lamb shoulder

2 Tbsp yellow mustard

2 Tbsp Rendered Lard (pg 294)

Tortillas (pg 334)

SUGGESTED TOPPINGS

Pico de Gallo (pg 254)

Guacamole

Radish slices

Fresh cilantro leaves

Fresh lime juice

In a small mixing bowl, combine all of the ingredients for the spice mix and stir to evenly combine.

Pour the water into a slow cooker and turn the heat to high. Cover the lamb shoulder with the mustard, then evenly distribute the spice mix all over the lamb. Make sure to get it into all of the crevices as best you can.

Heat the lard in a heavy skillet over medium to medium-high heat. The lard should be very hot, but not smoking. Sear the lamb on all sides to give it a golden brown crust. Place the lamb in the slow cooker, cover, and cook on high for 4 hours.

About 20 minutes before the lamb has finished cooking, prepare the tortillas.

When fully cooked, the lamb should shred easily with a fork. Remove the lamb from the slow cooker and shred it.

Top each tortilla with the shredded lamb and garnish with the toppings of your choice.

lamb chops with maple balsamic glaze

Serves: 4   Prep time: **10 minutes, plus 1–4 hours to marinate**   Cook time: **30 minutes**

· Nut-free   · Egg-free   · Nightshade-free

12 lamb rib chops, about 3/4 inch thick

MARINADE

1/4 cup coconut aminos

1/4 cup maple balsamic vinegar (see Notes)

1 tsp fresh lemon juice

1 tsp garlic powder

1 tsp dried oregano

Pinch of sea salt and ground black pepper

1 Tbsp cooking fat of choice

1 Tbsp unsalted grass-fed butter

Rinse the lamb chops under cool water and pat dry with a paper towel. Place the chops in a large sealable container or zip-top plastic bag. In a small mixing bowl, whisk together all of the ingredients for the marinade. Pour the marinade over the chops and seal the container. Place in the refrigerator to marinate for at least 1 hour, ideally 4 hours.

Preheat the oven to 375°F. Remove the lamb chops from the marinade and allow them to come to room temperature. Reserve the marinade. Heat a large cast-iron skillet over medium-high heat and melt the cooking fat in the skillet. Sear the chops until browned on both sides, about 5 minutes total. Place the skillet in the oven for 2 minutes for medium-rare chops. Remove the chops from the oven and allow to rest.

To make the glaze, pour the reserved marinade into a small saucepan. Add the butter and reduce over medium-low heat, stirring continuously, until the sauce starts to reduce and thicken, about 10 minutes.

To serve, place the chops on a platter and drizzle with the glaze.

Cook's Notes:

If you can't find maple balsamic vinegar, you can use plain balsamic vinegar and add 1–2 tsp of maple syrup or granulated maple sugar to the marinade. This marinade is perfect for pork chops and chicken as well.

You can also grill the chops instead of pan-frying them.

lamb gyros with tzatziki sauce

Serves: **8**   Prep time: **30 minutes**   Cook time: **35 minutes**

• Nut-free

" Lamb with gyro seasoning is one of my all-time favorite flavor profiles. However, what takes gyro meat from good to great is the addition of tzatziki sauce. Hayley and I got to spend a little vacation time in Greece this past spring on an amazing trip through Europe, and we experienced Greek cuisine like never before. One way to make this dish easy for weeknight meals is to skip the tortillas and serve it directly over a big salad. "

Tzatziki (pg 266)

GYRO SPICE BLEND

1 Tbsp dried oregano

1 tsp dried marjoram

1 tsp dried thyme

1/2 tsp ground cumin

1/2 tsp sea salt

1/2 tsp ground black pepper

2 lbs ground lamb

1/2 Vidalia onion, minced

1 Tbsp minced garlic

Tortillas (pg 334)

TOPPINGS

1/2 cup sliced cucumber

1/2 cup sliced cherry tomatoes

1/4 cup minced red onion

1 cup baby lettuce

Chopped fresh dill, for garnish (optional)

Prepare the tzatziki and refrigerate until ready to use.

Preheat the oven to 350°F. Place all of the ingredients for the spice blend in a small mixing bowl and stir to combine. Place the ground lamb in a large mixing bowl and top with the spice blend, onion, and garlic. Using your hands, knead all of the ingredients together to combine.

Shape the meat into a loaf and place on a rimmed baking sheet. Bake for 25–30 minutes, or until the internal temperature reaches 155°F.

While the meat is baking, prepare the tortillas.

When the internal temperature of the meat reaches 155°F, remove it from the oven and turn the oven to broil on high. Slice the meat into thin strips and arrange them on the rimmed baking sheet. Broil for 3 minutes, flip the meat, and broil for 3 minutes on the other side, draining the fat from the baking sheet as necessary.

To serve, top each tortilla with gyro meat, a few slices of cucumber, a few slices of tomato, a sprinkle of red onion, a few pieces of baby lettuce, and a dollop of tzatziki. Garnish with fresh dill, if desired.

Cook's Note:

To make this recipe dairy-free, make the tzatziki using coconut milk yogurt. To make this recipe nightshade-free, simply omit the cherry tomatoes from the toppings.

moroccan short ribs

Serves: **2**   Prep time: **20 minutes**   Cook time: **2 1/2 hours**

· Dairy-free   · Nut-free   · Egg-free

 " This dish is a favorite of ours. It is easy to prepare and fills the house with a wonderful aroma while it slowly cooks. There are two parts to this recipe that make it decidedly Moroccan: cooking it in a tagine and using a spice blend called Ras el Hanout. If you don't have a tagine (that red thing in the photo), you can cook it in a slow cooker or Dutch oven (don't worry, no one will ever know). However, I strongly recommend sticking to the spice blend. Ras el Hanout is a signature flavor in Moroccan cuisine. If you can't find it at your local grocery store, we have a recipe to make it yourself on pg 273. "

2 Tbsp duck fat

Sea salt

1 1/2 lbs beef short ribs

1 Tbsp plus 1 tsp Ras el Hanout (pg 273), divided

2 carrots, peeled and sliced

1/4 large yellow onion, chopped

1 1/2 cups diced fresh tomatoes

1 cup Chicken Stock (pg 278)

2 cloves garlic, smashed with the side of a knife

1 bay leaf

Juice of 1/2 lemon (1 1/2 Tbsp)

1/2 tsp ground turmeric

1/2 tsp sea salt

1/2 tsp ground black pepper

Place the duck fat in a tagine or Dutch oven over medium-high heat. Liberally salt the short ribs and sear them for 2 minutes on each side (8–10 minutes total). Slide the tagine off the heat and remove the ribs to a rimmed baking sheet. Season the ribs with 1 Tbsp of the Ras el Hanout.

Preheat the oven to 350°F. Return the tagine to the burner, add the carrots and onion, and sauté over medium heat for 2 minutes. Add the tomatoes, stock, garlic, bay leaf, lemon juice, turmeric, salt, pepper, and remaining 1 tsp of Ras el Hanout. Stir to combine and simmer for a few minutes.

Return the ribs to the pot, nestling them into the vegetables. Cover with a tight-fitting lid and place in the oven for 2 1/2 hours, until the meat is tender and falling off the bone.

nightshade-free breakfast sausage

Serves: **4–6**   Prep time: **15 minutes**   Cook time: **15 minutes**

· Dairy-free   · Nut-free   · Egg-free   · Nightshade-free

 " I love to have sausage on my brunch or breakfast menu. Typically seasoned with paprika and often red pepper flakes or cayenne pepper, breakfast sausage is often off-limits to those who can't eat nightshades. I created this recipe so that those of you who avoid nightshades can still enjoy the wonderful flavors of breakfast sausage! "

1 tsp sea salt

1 tsp garlic powder

1 tsp onion powder

1 tsp dried oregano

1/2 tsp ground black pepper

1/4 tsp ground white pepper

1/4 tsp rubbed sage

1/4 tsp ground turmeric

1/4 tsp ground cinnamon

1 lb ground pork

1 Tbsp Rendered Lard (pg 294) or other cooking fat of choice

Combine the salt and spices in a small mixing bowl.

Place the ground pork in a large mixing bowl. Add the spice mixture and thoroughly knead the spices into the pork with your hands. Form the seasoned pork into about 12 small (1- to 2-oz) patties.

Heat the lard in a medium-sized cast-iron skillet over medium heat. Place several of the patties in the hot pan, spaced apart so they cook evenly. Cook the patties for 2–3 minutes on each side, or until they are golden brown on the outside and no longer pink in the middle. Repeat with the remaining patties.

Serve alongside your favorite breakfast foods.

porcini-crusted lamb chops

Serves: **2–4**   Prep time: **20 minutes**   Cook time: **25 minutes**

· Dairy-free   · Nut-free   · Egg-free   · Nightshade-free

10 lamb rib chops, about 1 inch thick

1/4 cup packed fresh rosemary leaves

1 cup (1 oz) dried porcini mushrooms

2 cloves garlic

1/4 cup extra-virgin olive oil, plus more for drizzling

Sea salt and ground black pepper

Preheat the oven to 425°F. Rinse the lamb chops under cold water and pat dry with a paper towel.

Place the rosemary, mushrooms, and garlic in a food processor or mini food chopper. Pulse until you have a moderately coarse and even consistency to coat the lamb chops, about 30 seconds.

Pour the mushroom mixture onto a plate. Pour the olive oil into a small mixing bowl and set out a clean plate for the lamb.

Lightly dip a lamb chop into the olive oil and then press each side of the chop into the mushroom mixture. Place the coated chop on the clean plate and season with salt and pepper. Repeat with the remaining chops.

Place the lamb chops in an ovenproof skillet or on a rimmed baking sheet lined with parchment paper, lightly drizzle with olive oil, and bake for 20–25 minutes, until the center of the chops reaches 140°F for medium doneness.

pork and apple ravioli

Yield: **18 ravioli**   Prep time: **45 minutes**   Cook time: **20 minutes**

• Dairy-free

Red Sauce with a Kick (pg 258)

FILLING

1 Tbsp Rendered Lard (pg 294)

1/3 cup chopped onion

1/2 cup peeled and diced green apple

1/2 cup portobello mushrooms, diced

7 fresh sage leaves, minced

1/2 tsp sea salt

1/4 tsp ground black pepper

1/2 lb ground pork

2 (12-oz) packages Cappello's grain-free lasagna sheets (see Notes)

Prepare the red sauce and keep warm while preparing the ravioli.

Make the filling: In a medium-sized skillet over medium heat, melt the lard. Add the onion and sauté until lightly caramelized, about 5 minutes. Add the apple, mushrooms, sage, salt, and pepper and continue to sauté until the apple and mushrooms have softened, approximately 10–12 minutes. Add the ground pork and cook until the pork is no longer pink. Set aside to cool.

Assemble the ravioli: Have a small bowl of water nearby. Work with pairs of lasagna sheets, designating one as a bottom sheet and one as a top sheet. These will be stuck together with the filling in the middle.

On the bottom sheet, place three 1-Tbsp portions of filling, spaced evenly, leaving room for the edges of the dough to be pressed together. With the water, use your finger to wet an outline around each portion of the filling, which will allow the top sheet to adhere. Place the top sheet over the bottom sheet and press down around each pocket of filling where you wet the dough. When bringing the sheets together, try to eliminate any air pockets around the filling. Repeat this process until you run out of sheets or filling.

Using a pastry wheel or pizza cutter, cut around the filling pockets, leaving approximately a 1/4-inch border, to create the individual ravioli.

Bring a salted pot of water to a rolling boil and carefully drop in the ravioli, 3 or 4 at a time. Cook for 3 minutes, or until soft and tender. Strain the ravioli from the water and place on a drying rack before plating. Repeat this process with the rest of the ravioli, allowing the water to come back up to a boil between batches.

Serve the ravioli topped with the red sauce.

Cook's Notes:

The filling can also be used as a meat sauce for squash noodles. In place of Cappello's lasagna sheets, you can use Wrapper Dough (pg 336) or Nut-Free Pasta Dough (pg 328).

pork chops with apple chutney

Serves: **4**   Prep time: **15 minutes**   Cook time: **45 minutes**

· Dairy-free   · Nut-free   · Egg-free

APPLE CHUTNEY

5 Granny Smith apples, peeled and diced

2 cloves garlic, minced

1/2 red onion, finely chopped

1 cup granulated maple sugar

Juice of 1 orange

1 cup apple cider vinegar

1 Tbsp grated fresh ginger

1 Tbsp red pepper flakes

4 bone-in pork chops, about 1 inch thick

Sea salt

Combine all of the ingredients for the chutney in a medium-sized saucepan. Bring to a boil over medium-high heat, then reduce the heat to low. Simmer for 30–40 minutes, until the apples are soft and the liquid has reduced by one-quarter. Set aside to cool.

Preheat a grill to 500°F (medium-high). While the grill is heating, remove the pork chops from the refrigerator. Pat dry with a paper towel and season with salt. Grill the pork chops until the desired internal temperature is reached. We typically grill 1-inch-thick pork chops for 10–12 minutes, until they are no longer pink in the middle and the internal temperature reaches 160°F.

Serve the chops topped with the apple chutney.

Cook's Note:

Because it is vinegar-based, the chutney will keep for up to 2 weeks in the refrigerator.

pork dumplings

Serves: **4**   Prep time: **30 minutes, plus 1–2 hours to marinate**   Cook time: **30 minutes**

· Dairy-free

FILLING

1 lb ground pork

1 tsp grated fresh ginger

1 Tbsp coconut aminos

4 cloves garlic, minced

1/2 tsp sea salt

7 grinds black pepper

1/4 cup minced cabbage

2 Tbsp thinly sliced scallions

1 large egg, whisked

Dumpling Sauce (pg 240)

1 1/2 batches Wrapper Dough (pg 336)

In a medium-sized mixing bowl, combine the ground pork, ginger, coconut aminos, garlic, salt, and pepper. Cover and place in the refrigerator to marinate for 1–2 hours.

Before assembling the dumplings, make the Dumpling Sauce and set aside until ready to use.

Bring a large pot of salted water to a rolling boil. Using your hands, combine the marinated pork with the cabbage, scallions, and whisked egg. Form the pork mixture into small balls, about 1 Tbsp per ball.

Drop 6–10 balls at a time into the boiling water and boil for 7 minutes. Remove the cooked balls from the pot and set aside to cool. Repeat until all of the meatballs have been boiled, allowing the water to come back up to a boil between batches.

Make the Wrapper Dough and roll it out between two sheets of parchment paper to a thickness of about 1/8 inch. Cut out circular wrappers with a 3 3/4-inch round cookie cutter or mason jar lid.

Place a cooked meatball in the center of each wrapper. Bring the dough up around the meatball, pinching and folding it at the top to close it.

Prepare a pot with a steamer basket, greasing the metal basket with the cooking fat of your choice. If using a bamboo basket, line it with parchment. Steam the dumplings in the steamer basket for 10 minutes. Serve the dumplings with the Dumpling Sauce.

Cook's Note:

If you can't eat nuts, substitute Nut-Free Pasta Dough (pg 328) for the Wrapper Dough.

pork meatballs with creamy sauce

Serves: **4–6**   Prep time: **35 minutes**   Cook time: **35 minutes**

· Dairy-free   · Nut-free   · Egg-free

CREAM SAUCE

1 Tbsp ghee, store-bought
or homemade (pg 286)

1/2 Vidalia onion, diced

2 cloves garlic, smashed
with the side of a knife
and minced

1 (5.4-oz) can coconut cream

1 1/2 cups Chicken Stock
(pg 278)

Sea salt and ground black
pepper

1/2 cup chopped celery

6 white mushrooms, sliced

3 Roma tomatoes, seeded
and diced

MEATBALLS

1 1/2 lbs ground pork

1/2 tsp sea salt

5 grinds black pepper

1 1/2 tsp dried oregano

1/2 tsp dried marjoram

1/2 loosely packed cup
fresh parsley leaves,
chopped

1/2 tsp red pepper flakes

1/4 tsp onion powder

1/4 tsp garlic powder

1 large egg, whisked
(optional)

1 Tbsp Rendered Lard
(pg 294)

2 white sweet potatoes,
peeled and spiral-sliced

Make the sauce: Heat the ghee in a 5 1/2-quart enameled Dutch oven. Add the onion and garlic and sauté until fragrant, about 2 minutes. Stir in the coconut cream. Add the stock to the pot and stir until evenly combined. Season with salt and pepper and reduce the heat to medium-low. Allow the sauce to slowly reduce, stirring every so often.

Once the sauce has started to thicken, add the celery and mushrooms and cook for 5 minutes. Add the tomatoes, stir to combine, and cook for 5 additional minutes. Reduce the heat to low and simmer, uncovered, while you make the meatballs.

In a medium-sized mixing bowl, combine the ground pork with the salt, pepper, oregano, marjoram, parsley, red pepper flakes, onion powder, and garlic powder. Knead the mixture with your hands until the spices are evenly blended into the meat. Add the whisked egg (if using) to the meat mixture and knead again to combine.

Form the meat mixture into 1- to 2-oz meatballs (about the size of a golf ball) and set aside. Heat the lard in a cast-iron skillet over medium-high heat. Sear the meatballs until browned on all sides, about 8–10 minutes total. Add the seared meatballs to the sauce and continue to simmer until the meatballs are cooked through, about 20 minutes.

While the meatballs are simmering in the sauce, prepare the sweet potato noodles. Place the spiral-sliced sweet potatoes in a large, heatproof glass mixing bowl. Bring enough water to cover the noodles to a rolling boil in a large pot. Once the water comes to a boil, remove the pot from the heat and pour the water over the noodles, making sure that the noodles are fully submerged. Cover the bowl with a lid and let the noodles sit in the hot water for 20 minutes, or until tender. Drain the noodles and serve topped with the meatballs and sauce.

ramen with chashu and marinated eggs

❝ Comfort food, street food, food with a fan following, food to eat with your family: Call it what you like—just don't call it Top Ramen. This dish is extremely popular with anyone who loves Japanese cuisine. I learned how to make ramen from Chef Matt Kemp. Although this recipe is far from traditional ramen, I still used techniques learned from him for this grain-free version of the dish. I recommend using kelp noodles (found in most health-oriented grocery stores) because they hold their shape so well. If you are okay with white rice, you can purchase rice noodles instead. Otherwise, using sweet potato noodles or zucchini noodles is a great way to add more vegetables to this dish. Feel free to get creative with extra toppings as well. Note that this recipe yields more eggs than required for the Ramen. However, the eggs are great by themselves or as an on-the-go snack! They can be stored in the fridge for up to 5 days. ❞

chashu

Yield: **16 oz pork belly**   Prep time: **15 minutes**   Cook time: **2 hours**

· Dairy-free   · Nut-free   · Egg-free   · Nightshade-free

2 (8-oz) pieces pork belly

Sea salt and ground black pepper

1 (8-oz) bottle coconut aminos

1/4 cup granulated maple sugar

7 cloves garlic

1 (2-inch) piece of fresh ginger, sliced

5 scallions

1 shallot, quartered

1/4 cup balsamic vinegar

1/4 cup white wine vinegar

Heat a large cast-iron skillet over medium-high heat. Sprinkle the pork belly with salt and pepper. Sear each side for 1–2 minutes, until golden brown. For thicker pieces of belly, double the sear time.

Remove the belly from the heat and place it in a slow cooker with the rest of the ingredients. Add enough water to cover the belly by 1 inch and cook on high for 1 hour, then on low for 1 hour.

The pork belly can be served as is, but if using for ramen (opposite), place the belly and liquid in the refrigerator until completely cool. Slicing the pork belly when it's cool helps keep its shape and creates cleaner cuts.

marinated eggs

Yield: **12 eggs**   Prep time: **15 minutes, plus 2 hours to chill**   Cook time: **1 hour 10 minutes**

· Dairy-free   · Nut-free   · Nightshade-free

MARINADE

2 medium purple beets

1 cup white wine vinegar

1 Tbsp granulated maple sugar

1/2 Tbsp ground cloves

2 Tbsp grated fresh ginger

1 tsp onion powder

1 tsp garlic powder

2 Tbsp balsamic vinegar

12 large eggs

Wash the beets well under cool water and place in a medium-sized saucepan. Cover with water and boil until the beets are fork-tender, about 45 minutes. Once the beets have cooled, peel the skins, place the beets in a food processor or high-speed blender, and purée until smooth. Pour the puréed beets into a large glass container with a lid. Add the white wine vinegar, maple sugar, cloves, ginger, onion powder, garlic powder, and balsamic vinegar and stir to combine.

Bring a medium-sized pot of water to a rolling boil. Gently poke a hole in the tip of each egg. Place 3 eggs in the water and boil for 6 minutes. Remove and immediately place in a bowl of ice water. Allow the pot of water to come back up to a roiling boil and continue this process until all of the eggs are cooked.

Carefully peel the eggs, place in the marinade, cover, and refrigerate for at least 2 hours. Rinse the eggs and eat, or add to a bowl of ramen.

ramen

Serves: **4**   Time needed: **30 minutes**

· Dairy-free   · Nut-free   · Nightshade-free

4 cups Chicken Stock (pg 278)

1 1/2 cups Chashu liquid

1 Tbsp sea salt

8 grinds black pepper

4 Marinated Eggs

Chashu

Kelp noodles, spiral-sliced sweet potato noodles, or spiral-sliced zucchini noodles

Grilled scallions or bok choy

2 sheets nori, cut into squares, for garnish

Combine the stock and Chashu liquid in a large pot. Add the salt and pepper. Turn on the heat to medium and simmer for 15 minutes.

Slice the Chashu (pork belly) crosswise into 1/4-inch slices.

In a saucepan, bring a serving's worth of the blended broth (about 1 1/4 cups) to a low simmer. Add one-quarter of the sliced pork belly and simmer until the belly is warm. Pour into a serving bowl over noodles. Slice a marinated egg in half and place in the bowl. Add other vegetables, such as grilled scallions or perhaps bok choy, to create a hardy and filling bowl of soup. Garnish with squares of nori. Repeat with the remaining ingredients to make 4 servings.

scottish meat pies

Serves: **4**   Prep time: **45 minutes**   Cook time: **15 minutes**

❝ Probably one of my all-time favorite foods, meat pies are the perfect meal for a cold night. This dish definitely will not disappoint those of you who miss savory pies. If you don't enjoy the taste of offal, the beef liver in this recipe can be omitted, but it is mild and well incorporated for those of you needing to get more superfoods into your diet. ❞

Savory Chestnut Flour Pie Crusts (pg 332)

FILLING

1 Tbsp Rendered Lard (pg 294) or other cooking fat of choice

1/2 yellow onion

4 cloves garlic

1/2 bulb fennel

1 lb ground beef

1/2 lb ground pork

1 oz (1/4 cup) finely chopped beef liver (optional)

Sea salt and ground black pepper

1/2 tsp curry powder

1/2 tsp rubbed sage

1/2 tsp ground white pepper

1/2 tsp dried thyme

1/4 tsp ground cinnamon

3/4 cup Beef Stock (pg 278)

1/2 cup grass-fed heavy cream or coconut cream

1 sweet potato, peeled and diced

1 cup diced mushrooms

1 large egg

Prepare four single-serving pie crusts and bake them for 10 minutes. Set aside while you make the filling.

Place the lard in a large skillet over medium heat and sauté the onion, garlic, and fennel until the onion is soft and translucent. Add the beef, pork, and beef liver (if using) to the skillet and cook until browned. Add salt and black pepper to taste, along with the curry powder, sage, white pepper, thyme, and cinnamon, and stir to combine. Sauté for 1 more minute, then remove from the heat and set aside.

In a saucepan over medium heat, combine the stock, heavy cream, sweet potato, and mushrooms. Simmer until the sweet potato is nearly soft. Add the meat mixture and allow the mixture to reduce and thicken.

Preheat the oven to 350°F. Once the filling has reduced, scoop it into the prebaked pie crusts. Using a dab of water, wet the rims of the crusts, drape the second layer of pie crust on top, and gently crimp the edges to attach. Whisk the egg and brush the tops of the pies with it. Bake the pies for 12–15 minutes, until golden brown.

smoked ribs

Serves: **2**   Prep time: **30 minutes**   Cook time: **4 1/2 hours to smoke or 50 minutes to grill**

· Dairy-free   · Nut-free   · Egg-free

 66Our mild obsession with smoked meats and barbecue started when we first visited Texas. Upon returning home, it became our mission to seek out places to get authentic barbecue, though our options were decidedly limited in Pittsburgh. Then last year we got a small smoker! This recipe is the way we make ribs in our smoker, though the smoking step is optional. You can also prepare these ribs on the grill. 99

1 (3-lb) rack pork spareribs

1 1/2 Tbsp yellow mustard

RUB

2 Tbsp coconut sugar

1 1/2 tsp paprika

1 tsp garlic powder

1 tsp onion powder

1 tsp pink Himalayan salt

1/2 tsp ground cumin

1/2 tsp dried oregano

1/4 tsp ground white pepper

1/4 tsp chipotle powder

Smoky Barbecue Sauce
(pg 262)

1/4 cup pure apple juice

Remove the ribs from the refrigerator 30 minutes prior to smoking and allow them to come to room temperature. Remove the silver skin from the underside of the ribs. Cover the ribs evenly with the yellow mustard.

Mix together the rub ingredients in a small mixing bowl. Evenly distribute the rub over the ribs, using more of the rub on the meaty top side.

Place the ribs in a smoker on a low heat setting (around 220°F), which will apply the most smoke. Allow the ribs to smoke for 3 hours. After 2 hours, start preparing the Smoky Barbecue Sauce.

After 3 hours, remove the ribs from the smoker and place them on a sheet of foil. Before sealing the ribs in the foil, pour in the apple juice. Wrap the ribs tightly, then place them back on the smoker for an additional 90 minutes on a medium heat setting (about 300°F).

Serve the ribs with a coating of barbecue sauce, or serve the sauce on the side.

Cook's Note:

If you are planning to use a grill for this recipe, start off by preparing the barbecue sauce. Parboil the ribs in a large stockpot for 30 minutes (if you are unsure of how to do it, this method is described on pg 74). Once the ribs have cooled slightly, cover them with the mustard and spices. Heat your grill to medium-low and grill the ribs while brushing with the barbecue sauce. Once the ribs have developed some character from the sauce caramelizing, give them one final brushing with the sauce and serve.

poultry & eggs

asian chicken salad

Serves: 6 as a side, 3 as a main   Prep time: **30 minutes, plus 1–3 hours to marinate**   Cook time: **12–16 minutes**

• Dairy-free   • Nightshade-free

MARINADE

1/2 cup coconut aminos

1 Tbsp toasted sesame oil

1 tsp fish sauce

1/2 tsp sea salt

1/2 tsp ground black pepper

4 cloves garlic, smashed with the side of a knife

1 Tbsp minced fresh ginger

2 scallions, roughly chopped

3 boneless, skinless chicken breasts (about 1 1/2 lbs)

6 cups mixed salad greens (1 cup per serving for side portions, 2 cups per serving for main portions)

2 medium carrots, peeled and julienned

3 mandarin oranges, peeled and sectioned

1 small bunch enoki mushrooms

1 small daikon radish, julienned

Fried Wontons (pg 322)

Cilantro Ginger Dressing (pg 236)

In a medium-sized mixing bowl, whisk together all of the ingredients for the marinade.

Rinse the chicken under cold water and pat dry with a paper towel. Place the chicken in a sealable container or zip-top plastic bag container with the marinade, toss to coat, and refrigerate for 1–3 hours.

Remove the chicken from the refrigerator and allow it to come to room temperature. Preheat a grill to medium (400°F). Place the chicken on the hot grates and cook until it is no longer pink in the middle, 12–16 minutes, depending on thickness. (Discard the marinade.) Remove from the grill and allow to cool.

Cut the cooled chicken into 1/2-inch cubes.

Assemble the salad by placing salad greens in each salad bowl. Top the greens with the chicken, julienned carrots, orange sections, mushrooms, daikon, and wontons. Drizzle with the dressing and serve.

Cook's Note:

To make this recipe nut-free, follow the nut-free variation for the wontons using the Nut-Free Pasta Dough (pg 328).

baked eggs with spaghetti squash

Serves: **4–6**   Prep time: **50 minutes**   Cook time: **25 minutes**

• Dairy-free   • Nut-free

1 large spaghetti squash

1 cup Red Sauce with a Kick (pg 258; see Note)

4 to 6 large eggs

Sea salt and ground black pepper

1/2 tsp dried oregano

Place an oven rack in the second highest position, and preheat the oven to 375°F.

Slice the ends off the spaghetti squash, then slice the squash lengthwise down the center. Scoop out the seeds, then place the squash halves on a large rimmed baking sheet, cut side up. Bake the squash for 40–45 minutes, until the squash is tender and the "noodles" can easily be shredded with a fork. While the squash is cooking, prepare the red sauce.

Let the squash cool before shredding the noodles by scraping a fork along the inside. Place the squash noodles in a medium-sized ovenproof skillet and pour the red sauce over the squash.

Using a spoon or spatula, create 4–6 little "nests" in the squash, one for each egg. Crack the eggs, one at a time, into a small ramekin, and pour an egg into each nest. This is the best way to add the eggs without the risk of breaking a yolk.

Sprinkle the tops of the eggs with salt, pepper, and oregano. Bake for about 25 minutes, until the whites of the eggs are fully cooked. (The timing will vary depending on the temperature of your oven.)

Cook's Note:

If you want to take a shortcut, simply substitute a clean-ingredient tomato sauce for the Red Sauce with a Kick. You could also use a cup of crushed tomatoes and throw in some of the seasonings used in the red sauce recipe.

chicken en brodo

Serves: **2**   Prep time: **25 minutes**   Cook time: **35 minutes**

· Dairy-free   · Nut-free   · Egg-free   · Nightshade-free

 66 One of the dishes my mom made in regular rotation when I was growing up was chicken à la king, a chicken dish with a creamy white mushroom sauce and biscuits. This dish is a dairy-free spin on the old Staley family recipe. What makes this version great, in my opinion, is the richness of the mushroom sauce paired with crispy-skinned and perfectly seasoned chicken. This dish always feels like the perfect comfort food when the weather starts to cool off in the fall. 99

1 small (3-lb) chicken or Cornish game hen

Sea salt

1 1/2 Tbsp duck fat

1 1/4 cups Chicken Stock (pg 278), divided

Ground black pepper

4 cloves garlic, smashed with the side of a knife

1 shallot, sliced

1 Tbsp ghee, store-bought or homemade (pg 286)

1/2 lemon

1 tsp dried oregano

1 tsp grated lemon zest

4 cups sliced cremini mushrooms

Preheat the oven to 400°F. Rinse the chicken under cold water and pat dry with a paper towel.

Starting breast side up, cut the chicken down the center between the breasts, on either side of the backbone. Discard the back or save it for stock. Season the chicken halves with salt. Heat the duck fat in a 12-inch ovenproof skillet over medium-high heat. Add the chicken halves and sear on both sides until browned. Place the pan in the oven (with the chicken skin side up) and roast for 25 minutes. Remove from the oven and turn the temperature down to 325°F. Pour 1/2 cup of the stock over the chicken, season with pepper, and place back in the oven for 10 minutes, or until the internal temperature of the breast reaches 165°F.

Sauté the garlic and shallot in the ghee over medium heat until fragrant, and season with salt and pepper. Squeeze the lemon juice over the garlic and shallot, add the oregano and lemon zest, and stir. Add mushrooms and continue to sauté until tender. Add the remaining 3/4 cup of stock and bring to a bubble. Reduce the heat to low and simmer until the sauce has reduced by almost half.

Divide the sauce and mushrooms between two shallow bowls. Top each bowl with a chicken half and serve.

chicken salad with currants

Serves: **4**   Prep time: **30 minutes**   Cook time: **45 minutes**

• Dairy-free

4 bone-in, skin-on chicken thighs

3 heaping Tbsp Homemade Mayonnaise (pg 244)

1 heaping Tbsp dried currants

1/2 cup raw pecans, chopped

3 Tbsp thinly sliced scallions, plus more for garnish

Sea salt and ground black pepper

4 medium vine-ripened tomatoes

Rinse the chicken thighs under cold water and pat dry with a paper towel.

Preheat the oven to 400°F. Place the chicken, skin side up, in a rimmed baking dish. Bake for 45 minutes, then allow to cool completely (see Note).

Remove the skin from the chicken and shred the meat with 2 forks. Place the shredded chicken in a small mixing bowl. Add the mayonnaise and mix to coat the chicken evenly.

Add the currants, pecans, and scallions to the chicken mixture and season with salt and pepper. Stir again to make sure that the ingredients are evenly combined. Cover and place the salad in the fridge to keep it cool until ready to serve.

Carefully slice the tops off the tomatoes and scoop out the seeds with a spoon. Stuff each tomato with the chicken salad and garnish with additional scallions.

Cook's Notes:

Be sure that your shredded chicken is completely cool before adding the mayonnaise. Any heat coming from the chicken can cause the oils in the mayo to melt, in which case you will not get the classic creamy texture of chicken salad.

To make this recipe even easier, you can use leftover chicken from a previous meal, or purchase a high-quality rotisserie chicken from your local grocery store. Making chicken salad is one of our favorite ways to make use of leftover chicken.

chicken salsa salad

Serves: **4**   Prep time: **15 minutes**   Cook time: **20 minutes**

· Dairy-free   · Nut-free   · Egg-free

3 boneless, skinless chicken breasts (about 1 1/2 lbs)

Sea salt and ground black pepper

1 jalapeño

SALAD

1 red bell pepper, diced

1 green bell pepper, diced

2 vine-ripened tomatoes, seeded and diced

1 cup diced cucumbers

1/4 cup diced red onion

1/4 cup (a handful) fresh cilantro leaves, chopped

DRESSING

Juice of 2 limes (1/4 cup)

3 Tbsp extra-virgin olive oil

1 clove garlic, pressed

Dash of sea salt and ground black pepper

Rinse the chicken under cold water and pat dry with a paper towel.

Preheat a grill to medium heat (400°F). Season the chicken with salt and pepper. When the grill is hot, place the chicken and the whole jalapeño on the grill and reduce the heat to medium-low. Cook the chicken until it releases freely from the grill grate, about 8 minutes. Flip the chicken and cook the other side until the internal temperature in the thickest part of the breast reaches 165°F. Remove the chicken from the grill and allow to cool.

Move the jalapeño around while cooking to get a good char. When the jalapeño is char-grilled on the outside, the inside will be soft, with a smoky flavor. Remove from the grill and set aside. Once the jalapeño is cool, peel off all of the charred skin under cold running water. Slice the jalapeño in half and remove the seeds, then dice it.

Once the chicken is completely cool, dice it and set aside. Combine the bell peppers, tomatoes, cucumbers, and onion in a large salad bowl. Add the cilantro and stir to combine. Add the chicken and jalapeño and stir again to combine.

In a small mixing bowl, whisk together the ingredients for the dressing. Toss the salad in the dressing and serve.

chicken zoodle soup with meatballs

Serves: **8**   Prep time: **30 minutes**   Cook time: **1 hour**

· Dairy-free   · Nut-free   · Egg-free   · Nightshade-free

5 boneless, skinless chicken thighs

1 lb grass-fed ground beef

1 Tbsp adobo seasoning, store-bought or homemade (pg 272)

1 Tbsp ghee, store-bought or homemade (pg 286)

1/2 Vidalia onion, chopped

5 cloves garlic, sliced in half

2 qts Chicken Stock (pg 278)

1 bunch celery, chopped

4 carrots, peeled and chopped

1 Tbsp dried oregano

Sea salt and ground black pepper

1 head escarole, chopped

3 medium zucchini, spiral-sliced (see Notes)

Rinse the chicken under cold water, pat dry with a paper towel, and set aside.

Place the ground beef in a medium-sized mixing bowl. Using your hands, thoroughly mix the adobo seasoning into the beef. Form the seasoned beef into bite-sized meatballs and set aside.

In a large soup pot, warm the ghee over medium heat. Add the onion and garlic and sauté until the onion starts to become translucent. Pour in the stock, add the celery and carrots, and stir to combine. Add the chicken to the pot and season the soup with the oregano, salt, and pepper. Bring to a boil, then reduce the heat to low and simmer for 30 minutes.

Stir the escarole into the soup. Turn the heat back up to medium and, when the soup to starts to bubble again, add the meatballs, one at a time. Turn the heat back down to low and simmer until the meatballs are cooked through, about 20 minutes.

Add the zucchini noodles to the soup 10 minutes before serving so that they soften but do not become mushy.

Cook's Notes:

You can make this soup directly after making the stock. Simply strain the stock, then add the vegetables directly to the pot without sautéing them first. If you have the stock premade, then the extra step of sautéing the onion will add flavor to the soup!

If you don't own a spiral slicer, you can peel the zucchini into long strips using a julienne peeler for a similar effect.

hash brown nested eggs

Yield: **12 "nests"**   Prep time: **15 minutes**   Cook time: **25 minutes**

· Dairy-free   · Nut-free   · Nightshade-free

1 large sweet potato

Sea salt and ground black pepper

1 tsp nutritional yeast (optional; see Note)

1/4 cup coconut oil, plus more for the pan

12 large eggs

1-2 Tbsp finely sliced fresh chives

2 strips bacon, cooked and chopped

Place an oven rack in the second highest position, and preheat the oven to 375°F. Liberally grease a muffin tin with coconut oil.

Peel the sweet potato. Using the side of a box grater with the largest holes, grate the sweet potato. Place about 1/4 cup of the grated sweet potato in each muffin cup. Carefully press the sweet potato around the sides of the cup, creating a "nest." Make sure that the sides and bottom of each cup are evenly coated with sweet potato, adding a little extra to fill in any gaps.

Once all of the muffin cups are lined with shredded sweet potato, season each cup with a pinch each of salt, pepper, and nutritional yeast (if using). Melt the coconut oil, and, using a spoon, lightly drizzle it over the sweet potato nests. Bake the nests for 15 minutes, until the edges are crispy. Remove from the oven and allow to cool slightly.

Once the nests are cool, crack an egg into a small ramekin and gently pour the egg into a nest (this helps prevent the yolk from breaking) Repeat with the rest of the eggs. Sprinkle the eggs with a pinch of chives and some salt and pepper. Bake for 10–15 minutes, depending on how done you like your eggs.

Using a small offset spatula, carefully release the sides of the nests from the pan, then scoop out the nests with a spoon. Sprinkle with the bacon and serve.

Cook's Note:

The nutritional yeast adds a slightly cheesy flavor to the hash browns.

honey sesame wings

Serves: **4**   Prep time: **20 minutes**   Cook time: **25 minutes**

· Dairy-free   · Nut-free   · Egg-free

HONEY SESAME SAUCE

1/2 tsp coconut oil

1 tsp grated fresh ginger

1 tsp grated garlic

1/2 tsp red pepper flakes

1/4 cup coconut aminos

1/2 tsp fish sauce

1 Tbsp toasted sesame oil

1 Tbsp raw honey

24 chicken wings, cut into winglets

Sea salt

1 Tbsp sesame seeds, for garnish

1 scallion, thinly sliced, for garnish

Make the sauce: Heat the coconut oil in a small saucepan over medium-low heat. Add the ginger and garlic and sauté until fragrant. Add the red pepper flakes, coconut aminos, and fish sauce and stir to combine. Add the toasted sesame oil and honey and whisk over medium heat until the honey has completely dissolved and the sauce starts to bubble slightly. Reduce the heat to low and cook, stirring every so often, until the sauce has reduced and thickened enough to coat the back of a spoon. This can take up to 20 minutes.

While the sauce is reducing, grill the chicken wings. Preheat a grill to medium (400°F). Rinse the chicken under cold water, pat dry with a paper towel, and season with salt. Grill for 20–25 minutes, until cooked through, turning every 5 minutes. (Most grills have hot spots and cooler spots, so moving the chicken around a bit helps to ensure even cooking.)

Toss the chicken wings with the honey sesame sauce, sprinkle with the sesame seeds, and top with the sliced scallion.

Cook's Notes:

When reducing a liquid, low and slow is always best. It may take a little while to get there, but the time spent is worth it! A higher heat might reduce the sauce faster, but you risk burning and ruining your sauce.

You can also bake the wings at 400°F for 30 minutes instead of grilling them.

To make this recipe nightshade-free, omit the red pepper flakes.

lemongrass chicken curry

Serves: **4**   Prep time: **30 minutes**   Cook time: **1 1/2 hours**

· Dairy-free   · Nut-free   · Egg-free

2 Tbsp ghee, store-bought or homemade (pg 286), or coconut oil, divided

1/2 Vidalia onion, chopped

1 Tbsp minced fresh ginger

5 cloves garlic, sliced in half

Sea salt

1 heaping Tbsp green curry paste

1/4 tsp red pepper flakes

1 (13 1/2-oz) can full-fat coconut milk

1 cup Chicken Stock (pg 278)

1 Tbsp coconut aminos

1/4 tsp fish sauce

2 stalks dried lemongrass

5 bone-in, skinless chicken thighs

2 carrots, peeled and chopped

1 medium zucchini, chopped

1 red bell pepper, chopped

Basic Cauliflower Rice (pg 188)

In a medium-sized soup pot over medium heat, melt 1 Tbsp of the ghee. Add the onion and sauté until translucent. Add the ginger, garlic, and 1 tsp of salt and sauté for 1 minute. Add the curry paste and red pepper flakes and reduce the heat to medium-low. Add the coconut milk, stock, coconut aminos, fish sauce, and lemongrass. Reduce the heat to low, cover, and simmer for about 10 minutes.

Rinse the chicken thighs under cold water and pat dry with a paper towel. Add the chicken to the pot and turn the heat back up to medium-low. Cook for 15 minutes, then flip the chicken and cook for an additional 10 minutes.

Meanwhile, in a skillet over medium heat, sauté the carrots, zucchini, and bell pepper in about 1/2 Tbsp of the ghee. Season the vegetables with a pinch of salt.

After the chicken has cooked in the curry sauce for 25 minutes, add the sautéed vegetables to the pot and stir to combine all of the ingredients. Reduce the heat to low and let the sauce simmer for another 20 minutes, until it has reduced slightly (by about 1/2 inch to 1 inch).

While the sauce is simmering, make the cauliflower rice.

Remove the chicken from the sauce and shred it with two forks, if desired. Discard the bones. Also remove and discard the lemongrass stalks. Add the shredded chicken back to the sauce and stir to combine. To serve, plate the chicken curry over the cauliflower rice and enjoy.

orange chicken

Serves: **6**   Prep time: **25 minutes**   Cook time: **35 minutes**

• Dairy-free   • Nut-free

SAUCE

1 cup fresh orange juice

4 cloves garlic, minced

3 Tbsp coconut aminos

Juice of 1/2 lemon (1 1/2 Tbsp)

1 Tbsp raw honey

2 tsp coconut sugar

1 tsp grated fresh ginger

1/2 tsp red pepper flakes

1/2 tsp balsamic vinegar

1/2 cup filtered water or Chicken Stock (pg 278)

BATTER

1/4 cup coconut aminos

1 large egg, whisked

Up to 1 cup arrowroot starch

1 tsp sparkling water

2 cups duck fat or Rendered Lard (pg 294), for frying

8 boneless, skinless chicken thighs, rinsed and cut into chunks

Grated zest of 1 orange, for garnish

1 scallion, thinly sliced, for garnish

In a large saucepan over medium heat, combine all of the sauce ingredients. Bring to a boil, then reduce the heat to a simmer. Allow the sauce to reduce by one-quarter, about 10–15 minutes.

While the sauce is reducing, make the batter: Whisk together the coconut aminos and whisked egg. Slowly add the arrowroot starch until you have the consistency of a thick pancake batter. Gently stir in the sparkling water.

Place the duck fat in a heavy stockpot over medium-high heat, using a candy thermometer to monitor the temperature. When it reaches 375°F, dip the chunks of chicken into the batter and then place them in the hot fat in batches so as not to overcrowd the pot. Fry until fully cooked and crispy, about 4–6 minutes. Remove and allow to drain on a paper towel.

Toss the fried chicken with the sauce. Garnish with the orange zest and sliced scallion and serve.

pesto pasta with chicken

Serves: **6**   Prep time: **20 minutes**   Cook time: **30 minutes**

· Dairy-free   · Egg-free

Walnut Pesto or Nut-Free Pesto (pg 268)

6 boneless, skinless chicken thighs

1 Tbsp duck fat or Rendered Lard (pg 294)

Sea salt and ground black pepper

2 pinches of onion powder

4 large zucchini, peeled and spiral-sliced

1/2 cup quartered grape tomatoes

Prepare the pesto. Rinse the chicken thighs under cold water and pat dry with a paper towel.

Place the duck fat in a large cast-iron skillet over medium heat. Once the skillet is hot, add the chicken thighs. Sear them until they release freely from the skillet, about 3 minutes. Season with a pinch of salt and flip to sear the opposite side.

Season the browned side of the chicken with a pinch each of salt, pepper, and onion powder. Once the opposite side of the chicken releases freely, flip again, and season the other side with a pinch each of pepper and onion powder. Reduce the heat to medium-low and cook for 15 minutes, or until the chicken is no longer pink in the center.

While the chicken is cooking, steam the zucchini noodles in a steamer basket on the stovetop over medium heat until tender, about 13–15 minutes. Toss the steamed noodles with the pesto and quartered tomatoes.

Slice the chicken and serve over the zucchini noodles.

Cook's Note:

To make this recipe nut-free, use the Nut-Free Pesto (pg 268).

roasted chicken
with aromatic spices

Serves: **4**   Prep time: **15 minutes**   Cook time: **25 minutes per pound**

· Dairy-free   · Nut-free   · Egg-free

AROMATIC SPICE BLEND

1 tsp garlic powder

1 tsp onion powder

1 tsp dried oregano

1/2 tsp ground turmeric

1/2 tsp paprika

1/2 tsp sea salt

1/4 tsp chili powder

10 grinds black pepper

1 roasting chicken

1-2 Tbsp duck fat or ghee, store-bought or homemade (pg 286)

1/4 yellow onion

1/2 lemon

2 cloves garlic

Preheat the oven to 350°F.

In a small mixing bowl, combine all of the ingredients for the spice blend and stir until evenly combined.

Rinse the chicken, including the body cavity, under cold water and pat dry with a paper towel. Rub the skin of the bird with the duck fat.

Stuff the chicken with the onion, lemon, and garlic. Tie the legs together with kitchen twine and tuck the wings under the breast. Liberally season the bird with the spice blend. Place the chicken on a rack in a roasting pan and fill the bottom of the pan with 1/2 inch of water to prevent burning.

Roast the chicken for 25 minutes per pound, until the internal temperature in the breast reads 165°F and the juices run clear.

Cook's Notes:

If you can't elevate the chicken with a rack in the roasting pan, do not add water to the pan.

If the spices on the chicken start to burn, tent the chicken with foil until it is fully cooked.

roasted cornish game hens

Serves: **4**   Prep time: **15 minutes**   Cook time: **55 minutes**

• Dairy-free   • Nut-free   • Egg-free   • Nightshade-free

2 Cornish game hens

1 Tbsp duck fat

1 small lemon, cut in half
(see Notes)

1/4 Vidalia onion, cut in
half (see Notes)

Sea salt and ground black
pepper

1 cup Chicken Stock
(pg 278)

5 cloves garlic, smashed
with the side of a knife

Juice of 1/2 lemon (1 1/2
Tbsp)

Preheat the oven to 375°F. Rinse the game hens under cold water and pat dry with a paper towel, being sure to dry the body cavities as well.

Place the game hens in a roasting pan and liberally rub the skin with the duck fat, being sure to rub a good amount of the fat under the skin of the breast.

Stuff each hen with half a lemon and an eighth of an onion. Tuck the wings under the breast and tie the legs together with kitchen twine. Season the skin liberally with salt and pepper. Place in the oven and roast for 30 minutes.

While the hens are roasting, combine the stock, garlic, and lemon juice in a small mixing bowl. Stir and set aside.

After the hens have roasted for 30 minutes, remove them from the oven and pour the sauce mixture over the hens. Be sure that the garlic cloves sit in the liquid at the bottom of the pan and not on top of the birds. Place the hens back in the oven and roast for an additional 25 minutes, or until the internal temperature in the breast reaches 165°F and the skin is golden brown.

Cook's Notes:

These birds are very small, so you want to make sure that you can still tie the legs together when the birds are stuffed with the lemon and onion. Depending on the size of your lemon and onion, this will be anywhere from half a lemon to a quarter, and a quarter of an onion to an eighth.

You can baste the birds with the pan juices before they finish cooking. You can also whip the pan juices in a blender for a quick gravy to serve over the hens.

skillet chicken thighs

Serves: **4–6**   Prep time: **35 minutes**   Cook time: **25 minutes**

· Dairy-free   · Nut-free   · Egg-free   · Nightshade-free

 66Our good friend Pete is a talented chef, and he taught me how to remove the bones from chicken thighs and pan-sear them for a crispy and juicy chicken thigh dish. Ever since he taught me how to prepare chicken thighs this way, it has been my favorite way to enjoy chicken. Deboning thighs is a good skill to develop because boneless, skin-on thighs are not commonly available at the meat counter unless you request them from the butcher. Once the bones are removed, you sear the thighs skin side down for beautiful crispy skin, and when they release freely from the pan, they are ready to flip. This is an easy way to take simple chicken thighs and make them really spectacular!99

6 skin-on chicken thighs, bones removed (see Note)

Sea salt

1 tsp dried oregano

1/2 tsp garlic powder

1/2 tsp onion powder

10 grinds black pepper

1 (6-oz) jar artichoke hearts, drained and sliced

1 (4- to 5-oz) jar mixed Mediterranean olives, drained

2 Tbsp capers

1/2 lemon, sliced into rounds and quartered

Preheat the oven to 425°F.

Heat a large cast-iron skillet or other ovenproof skillet over medium heat. Rinse the chicken thighs under cold water and pat dry with a paper towel. Season the skin of the chicken thighs with salt and place them skin side down in the hot skillet. Flip the thighs once they release freely from the pan and have a nice brown sear on the skin.

Cook the chicken skin side up for 1 minute, then season evenly with the oregano, garlic powder, onion powder, and pepper. Add the artichoke hearts, olives, capers, and lemon slices to the skillet.

Place the skillet in the oven and roast for 25 minutes, until the chicken is fully cooked.

Cook's Note:

To remove the bone from a chicken thigh, simply run a paring knife along the side of the bone so that the meat separates easily from the bone. Continue to lightly roll the bone away from the meat with your opposite hand, while running your knife along the bone, one stroke at a time, until the meat is fully separated from the bone. You can freeze the thigh bones for future stock making.

spinach and artichoke quiche

Serves: **6**   Prep time: **30 minutes**   Cook time: **30–35 minutes**

• Dairy-free   • Nightshade-free

❝ When my aunt hosts a family brunch, quiche is always on her menu. It's a dish that can serve a lot of people, is beautiful to present to guests, and of course is delicious. This grain-free and dairy-free quiche is perfect for those who want to serve something elegant and tasty for brunch, or who just want to make a typical Sunday breakfast feel a little more special. ❞

Quiche Crust (pg 330)

1 Tbsp ghee, store-bought or homemade (pg 286)

1 shallot, diced

1 (6-oz) jar artichoke hearts, drained and chopped

1 cup sliced white mushrooms

1 tsp garlic powder

1/2 tsp dried thyme

Sea salt and ground black pepper

1 loosely packed cup baby spinach

6 large eggs

1/4 cup coconut cream

Prepare the crust and set it aside while you make the filling.

Preheat the oven to 350°F.

Heat the ghee in a large cast-iron skillet or other ovenproof skillet over medium heat. Add the shallot and sauté until translucent, about 3 minutes. Add the artichoke hearts, mushrooms, garlic powder, thyme, and a pinch each of salt and pepper. Sauté until the artichokes start to brown slightly and the mushrooms begin to soften. Add the baby spinach to the skillet and continue to sauté until the spinach starts to wilt slightly, about 30 seconds. Add more salt and pepper to taste, if needed. Remove the vegetables from the heat and allow them to cool to room temperature.

In a large mixing bowl, whisk the eggs until frothy. Add the coconut cream and whisk again until the cream is evenly combined with the eggs. Pour the cooled vegetables into the egg mixture and stir to combine. Pour the filling into the prepared crust and bake for 30–35 minutes, until the eggs are set.

stuffed chicken thighs

Serves: **4**   Prep time: **45 minutes**   Cook time: **35 minutes**

· Dairy-free   · Nut-free   · Egg-free

2 Tbsp ghee, store-bought or homemade (pg 286), divided

1/2 Vidalia onion, finely diced

1 (6-oz) jar artichoke hearts, drained and diced

1/2 cup diced sun-dried tomatoes

Sea salt and ground black pepper

1 1/2 packed cups baby spinach, chopped

8 boneless, skinless chicken thighs

1 1/4 cups Chicken Stock (pg 278), divided

Preheat the oven to 400°F.

Melt 1 Tbsp of the ghee in a large ovenproof skillet over medium heat. Add the onion and sauté until translucent. Add the artichoke hearts and tomatoes to the skillet and sauté until lightly browned. Season with salt and pepper to taste. Add the baby spinach and sauté until slightly wilted, about 30 seconds. Remove the vegetables from the heat and allow to cool. (Do not clean the skillet; you will be using it again.)

Rinse the chicken thighs under cold water and pat dry with a paper towel. On a sturdy cutting board, use a kitchen mallet to pound the chicken to a thin and even 1/4-inch thickness. Cut sixteen 8-inch lengths of kitchen twine, allowing two per thigh, and set aside.

Place about 1 Tbsp of the vegetable filling at one end of a chicken thigh and roll toward the other end. Use two pieces of cut twine to wrap the rolled thigh. Repeat this process until all of the chicken thighs are rolled and secured with twine. (You will have filling left over.)

Heat the remaining 1 Tbsp of ghee in the same skillet over medium-high heat. Sear the chicken thighs in the ghee for 6–8 minutes, rotating them as needed to brown evenly. Add 1/4 cup of the stock to the pan and then transfer the pan to the oven. Roast for 25 minutes or until the internal temperature in the thickest part of a thigh reaches 165°F.

While the chicken is roasting, reheat the remaining filling in a skillet over medium heat to serve with the chicken.

Remove the chicken from the pan and set aside to rest. Add the remaining 1 cup of stock to the pan and whisk over medium heat to reduce the sauce until thick, creating a nice pan-dripping gravy. Reduce the heat to low and keep the gravy warm until ready to serve. Serve the chicken over the remaining filling and drizzle with the warm gravy.

summer spring rolls with "peanut" sauce

Serves: **4**   Prep time: **30 minutes, plus 1–4 hours to marinate**   Cook time: **25 minutes**

· Dairy-free   · Nut-free   · Egg-free

5 boneless, skinless chicken thighs

MARINADE

1/4 cup coconut aminos

3 drops fish sauce

1/4 tsp garlic powder

1/4 tsp onion powder

1/4 tsp ground ginger

1/4 tsp red pepper flakes

Pinch of sea salt and ground black pepper

"Peanut" Sauce (pg 252)

1 Tbsp duck fat or other cooking fat of choice

1 cup sliced shiitake mushrooms

1 head green cabbage

3 medium carrots, peeled and julienned

1 medium daikon radish, julienned

1 avocado, thinly sliced

Rinse the chicken thighs under cold water and pat dry with a paper towel.

Mix together all of the marinade ingredients in a small mixing bowl. Place the chicken in a sealable container or zip-top plastic bag with the marinade. Refrigerate for at least 1 hour, or up to 4 hours.

Remove the chicken from the marinade and pat it dry with paper towels. Allow it to come to room temperature while you prepare the "Peanut" Sauce.

Heat the duck fat in a heavy skillet over medium-high heat. Sear the chicken on both sides, flipping as necessary to cook evenly. This should take 12–15 minutes. Transfer the chicken to a plate to cool. Once cool, slice it into 1/2-inch strips. Fry the mushrooms in the chicken juices until soft, then allow them to cool in the pan.

Peel 8 leaves from the head of cabbage and steam them in a large steamer basket or steamer pot until soft, about 10 minutes. Allow the leaves to cool enough that you can handle them. Wipe the excess water from each leaf and remove the thick stem from the center.

Preheat the oven to 350°F. Distribute the chicken, mushrooms, carrots, daikon, and avocado among the leaves. Drizzle each with a little sauce. Roll carefully, tucking in the sides when you get halfway to the end. Place the spring rolls in a baking dish and bake for 7–10 minutes, until warmed throughout.

Allow the rolls to cool slightly, then slice them in half. Serve with extra "Peanut" Sauce for dipping.

Cook's Note:

To make this recipe nightshade-free, omit the red pepper flakes.

thai fried chicken with tangy mango sauce

Serves: **4**   Prep time: **20 minutes, plus 3–4 hours to marinate**   Cook time: **30 minutes**

· Dairy-free   · Nut-free

 66 I've always been a huge fan of Thai cuisine, and I still get teased regularly at work for eating Thai food so often. Thai fried chicken is a perfect dish in my mind, and it is loved by all. The strong marinade in this recipe blends nicely with the light and crispy crust of the chicken. 99

4 boneless, skinless chicken breasts

MARINADE

1/4 cup plus 2 Tbsp fish sauce

3 Tbsp oyster sauce, store-bought or homemade (pg 250)

4 cloves garlic

1 Tbsp red pepper flakes

1/2 Tbsp minced fresh ginger

8 sprigs fresh cilantro, roughly chopped

1/2 tsp ground cumin

Pinch of sea salt and ground black pepper

Tangy Mango Sauce (pg 264)

2 cups duck fat, Rendered Lard (pg 294), or tallow, for frying

BATTER

2 large eggs, whisked

1 Tbsp coconut aminos

Up to 1 cup arrowroot starch

Rinse the chicken breasts under cold water and pat dry with a paper towel.

Combine all of the marinade ingredients in a small bowl. Put the chicken in a sealable container or zip-top plastic bag with the marinade, then place in the refrigerator to marinate for 3–4 hours.

Prepare the Tangy Mango Sauce and set it aside.

In a heavy saucepan, slowly bring the duck fat up to 375°F, using a candy thermometer to closely monitor the temperature.

While the fat is heating, prepare the batter. In a large mixing bowl, whisk together the eggs and coconut aminos. Slowly add the arrowroot starch until you have the consistency of a thick pancake batter.

When the fat reaches 375°F, dip the pieces of chicken into the batter and then place them in the hot fat in batches so as not to overcrowd the pot. Fry until fully cooked and crispy, about 4–6 minutes. Remove and allow to drain on a paper towel or wire rack over a baking sheet.

Serve the chicken with the Tangy Mango Sauce.

Cook's Note:

To make this recipe nightshade-free, omit the red pepper flakes.

tortilla española

Serves: **6**   Prep time: **25 minutes**   Cook time: **25 minutes**

· Dairy-free   · Nut-free   · Nightshade-free

1 medium white sweet potato

1 Tbsp plus 1 tsp duck fat, divided

1/2 Spanish onion, diced

8 large eggs

1/4 tsp garlic powder

1/2 tsp sea salt

10 grinds black pepper

3 Tbsp chopped fresh chives, plus more for garnish

Peel the sweet potato and slice it into 1/4-inch discs. Then cut the discs into quarters (pie-shaped).

Heat 1 Tbsp of the duck fat in a large skillet over medium heat. Sauté the sweet potato and onion in the duck fat until the sweet potato is soft and both ingredients are starting to brown, 20–25 minutes. Set aside and allow to cool slightly.

Preheat the oven to 350°F. In a medium-sized mixing bowl, whisk together the eggs, garlic powder, salt, pepper, and chives. Add the sweet potato and onion mixture and stir to combine.

Heat the remaining 1 tsp of duck fat in a 10-inch cast-iron skillet or other ovenproof stainless-steel skillet over medium heat until it just starts to bubble. Pour in the egg mixture and reduce the heat to medium-low. Cook for 10 minutes, then transfer the skillet to the oven and bake for 8 minutes.

Very carefully flip the "tortilla" (it's what most Americans would call a frittata at this point) by placing a large plate over the top of the skillet and flipping both at the same time, taking care to keep the plate pressed firmly against the skillet (and not burn yourself on the hot skillet).

Slide the tortilla back into the skillet with the uncooked side down. Finish cooking the tortilla on the stovetop over medium-low heat for 3 minutes. Slice and serve garnished with chives.

seafood

clam chowder

Serves: **4**   Prep time: **30 minutes**   Cook time: **30 minutes**

• Nut-free   • Egg-free

3 strips bacon, diced

1 yellow onion, diced

3 stalks celery, diced

3 cloves garlic, minced

1 1/2 cups Chicken Stock (pg 278)

1 cup bottled clam juice

2 Tbsp tomato puree

2 medium russet potatoes, peeled and diced

1/2 tsp sea salt

14 grinds black pepper

1/2 tsp paprika

1 (10-oz) can boiled baby clams, drained

1/2 cup grass-fed heavy cream or coconut cream

1 sprig fresh thyme, for garnish

In a Dutch oven over low heat, cook the bacon until the fat renders and the bacon starts to crisp. Add the onion and celery and raise the heat to medium-low. Cook the celery and onion with the bacon for approximately 15 minutes, then add the garlic. Continue cooking and stirring periodically for another 5–10 minutes, until the onion is translucent.

Add the stock, clam juice, tomato puree, potatoes, salt, pepper, and paprika. Cover and cook until the potatoes are fully cooked and soft, about 25 minutes.

Using an immersion blender, pulse the soup slightly to break up some of the solids and create a thicker soup.

Add the clams and cream to the soup. Mix together and bring to a simmer. Garnish with a sprig of fresh thyme and serve.

Cook's Note:

We use real grass-fed heavy cream for this recipe because it enhances the flavor of the chowder. If you cannot tolerate dairy, even grass-fed cream, you can substitute coconut cream. Just know that it will change the taste slightly, adding a hint of coconut flavor to the soup.

creamy crab bisque

Serves: **2–4**   Prep time: **20 minutes**   Cook time: **40 minutes**

· Nut-free   · Egg-free

1/2 Vidalia onion, chopped

3 cloves garlic, minced

2 Tbsp unsalted grass-fed butter

2 1/4 cups Chicken Stock (pg 278)

1 Tbsp tomato paste

1/4 tsp curry powder

2 medium carrots, peeled and chopped

1 cup grass-fed heavy cream

12 oz lump crab meat

Sea salt and ground black pepper

Chopped fresh chives, for garnish

In a large soup pot over medium heat, sauté the onion and garlic in the butter. When they begin to caramelize, add the stock, then whisk in the tomato paste.

When the tomato paste is fully incorporated into the stock, add the curry powder, carrots, and cream. Reduce the heat to low and cook, stirring regularly, until the bisque has thickened, approximately 30 minutes.

Add the crab meat and salt and pepper to taste. Simmer for an additional 7–10 minutes to warm the crab meat and allow the crab flavor to permeate the bisque.

Garnish with fresh chives and serve.

Cook's Note:

We use real grass-fed butter and cream for this recipe because they enhance the flavor of the bisque. If you cannot tolerate dairy, even grass-fed butter and cream, you can substitute ghee for the butter and coconut cream for the heavy cream. Just know that the coconut cream will change the taste slightly, adding a hint of coconut flavor to the soup.

fish tacos with smoky slaw

Serves: **4** Prep time: **45 minutes, plus 1–2 hours to marinate** Cook time: **3 minutes**

• Dairy-free • Nut-free

MARINADE

1/3 cup extra-virgin olive oil

1 Tbsp coconut aminos

1/2 tsp paprika

1/2 tsp dried dill

1/2 tsp onion powder

1 Tbsp fresh orange juice

1 1/2 lbs wild-caught yellowfin tuna steaks (see Note)

Tortillas (pg 334)

Smoky Slaw (pg 222)

Cilantro leaves, for garnish

Lime wedges, for garnish

In a mixing bowl, combine the marinade ingredients. Place the tuna steaks in a sealable container or zip-top plastic bag with the marinade, swirl to evenly coat the tuna, and refrigerate for 1–2 hours.

Prepare the tortillas and slaw.

Heat a heavy skillet over medium heat until hot. Lightly swirl a small amount of the cooking fat of your choice in the skillet. Sear the tuna on all sides, about 90 seconds per side.

Slice the seared tuna. Bring the dish together by plating slices of tuna over a tortilla. Top with some slaw, cilantro leaves, and a squeeze of lime juice.

Cook's Note:

Since the center of the tuna will be undercooked, purchasing good-quality fish is very important.

ginger suimono

Serves: **4**   Prep time: **10 minutes**   Cook time: **20 minutes**

· Dairy-free   · Nut-free   · Egg-free   · Nightshade-free

❝A suimono is a clear Japanese soup made for sipping. This dish is wonderful as a starter or an end to a meal. The ginger will help soothe your stomach after a rich meal. It's also perfect for anyone having trouble with appetite during times of illness.❞

2 cups Dashi (pg 284)

1 cup filtered water

1/2 Tbsp coconut aminos

1 (1-inch) piece ginger root, peeled and julienned

2 cloves garlic, thinly sliced

1/2 tsp sea salt

3 grinds black pepper

1 scallion, thinly sliced on the bias, divided

6 leaves bok choy

2 shiitake mushroom caps, julienned

1/2 sheet nori, cut into thin strips

In a medium-sized pot, combine the Dashi, water, coconut aminos, ginger, garlic, salt, pepper, half of the sliced scallion (reserve the rest for garnish), bok choy leaves, and mushroom caps. Bring to a low boil, then reduce the heat to medium-low and simmer for 20 minutes.

Pour into small sipping bowls and garnish with the remaining scallion and strips of nori.

Cook's Note:

For a stronger, more intense ginger presence, simmer the ginger root with the Dashi and water for an additional 10 minutes before adding the remaining ingredients.

lobster and avocado salad

Serves: **4**   Prep time: **20 minutes**   Cook time: **10 minutes**

· Dairy-free   · Nut-free   · Egg-free   · Nightshade-free

"In addition to being super fresh and delicious, this salad packs an interesting textural experience. I love the buttery and rich flavors of the lobster against the creamy chunks of avocado. The Lemon Vinaigrette is perfect for this salad, but you could experiment with other dressings as well. This salad is a great treat and a nice complement to a fancier summertime dinner."

4 (3-oz) lobster tails

2 ripe avocados, peeled and pitted

3 cups arugula

1/4 cup (a handful) fresh cilantro leaves, chopped

1 Tbsp chopped shallot

Lemon Vinaigrette (pg 248)

Sea salt and ground black pepper

1/4 cup microgreens

In a steamer basket set over a pot of boiling water, steam the lobster tails for 8–10 minutes, until the shells turn bright red and the meat is opaque. Once fully cooked, remove from the steamer basket and allow to cool.

Chop the avocados and place them in a glass mixing bowl. Add the arugula, cilantro, and shallot and carefully combine, being mindful not to mash the avocado. Drizzle the salad mixture with about 2 Tbsp of the vinaigrette and sprinkle with salt and pepper. Carefully toss to combine.

Remove the lobster meat from the shells and rinse the meat under cold water to be sure it is free of any shell pieces. Chop the meat into bite-sized chunks and set aside for plating.

Divide the dressed salad among four plates and top each with one-quarter of the steamed lobster meat. Lightly drizzle the lobster meat with additional vinaigrette, top with microgreens, and serve.

lobster fettuccine alfredo

Serves: **2**   Prep time: **25 minutes**   Cook time: **45 minutes**

· Dairy-free   · Egg-free

2 Tbsp ghee, store-bought or homemade (pg 286)

2 cloves garlic, smashed with the side of a knife and minced

2 tsp finely diced shallot

1/2 tsp sea salt

5 grinds black pepper

1 cup coconut cream

1/4 cup Chicken Stock (pg 278)

1 tsp nutritional yeast

4 small (2-oz) lobster tails

1 (12-oz) package Cappello's grain-free fettuccine or 2 large zucchini, spiral-sliced

1/2 cup quartered cherry tomatoes

1 Tbsp chopped fresh parsley

Heat the ghee in a small saucepan over medium heat. Add the garlic and shallot and sauté until translucent and fragrant, about 2 minutes. Turn the heat down to medium-low and season with the salt and pepper. Add the coconut cream and whisk until smooth.

Add the stock and nutritional yeast to the pot and continue to whisk until completely combined. Reduce the heat to low and allow the sauce to gently simmer and reduce while you prepare the rest of the dish, stirring every so often. The sauce is finished when it coats the back of a spoon, about 30–40 minutes.

Place the lobster tails in a steamer basket set over a pot of boiling water and steam for 8–10 minutes, or until the shells are bright red and the meat is opaque. Remove the cooked lobster tails from the pot and allow to cool.

While the lobster tails are steaming and cooling, prepare the noodles. If using Cappello's noodles, prepare according to the instructions on the packaging. If using spiral-sliced zucchini, steam the noodles until just tender, about 13–15 minutes.

Remove the lobster meat from the shells and rinse the meat under cold water to be sure it is free of any shell pieces. Chop the meat into bite-sized chunks and add it to the Alfredo sauce along with the tomatoes and parsley. Stir to combine evenly with the sauce. Plate the noodles, top with the lobster Alfredo, and serve.

Cook's Notes:

If you want the texture of real noodles but cannot have nuts, use Nut-Free Pasta Dough (pg 328) instead of the zucchini noodles.

To make this recipe nightshade-free, omit the cherry tomatoes.

pan-seared salmon
with avocado "cream" sauce

Serves: **4**   Prep time: **15 minutes**   Cook time: **15 minutes**

· Dairy-free   · Nut-free   · Egg-free   · Nightshade-free

 " This is a great recipe for beginner cooks and fish lovers. Simple and super fresh, this dish is a perfect summer meal after a long day. The trick to cooking the fish is to bring your pan fully up to heat before placing the fillets in it. This will sear the fillets to trap flavor and moisture. Don't try to move the fillets until they're ready, or you will likely tear the fish. When the fillets are ready to be flipped, they should lift easily from the pan, leaving you with beautifully crisp skin. "

AVOCADO "CREAM" SAUCE

1/4 cup coconut cream

1 avocado, peeled and pitted

2 tsp fresh lemon juice

1/4 tsp sea salt

3 grinds black pepper

1 clove garlic, chopped

1 Tbsp ghee, store-bought or homemade (pg 286)

4 skin-on salmon fillets, about 6 oz each

Sea salt and ground black pepper

Combine all of the sauce ingredients in a mini food processor or high-speed blender and blend until smooth.

In a large skillet over high heat, heat the ghee. Once the ghee is hot, reduce the heat to medium-low. Season the salmon on both sides with salt and pepper, place it skin side down in the hot pan, and cook for approximately 8 minutes. The skin should release easily from the pan.

Flip the salmon and cook it flesh side down for an additional 4 minutes. Carefully release the fish from the pan. It should lift easily; if it doesn't, it may need a little more time in the pan.

To serve, place a generous dollop of the Avocado "Cream" Sauce on each plate and top with the salmon.

salmon cakes
with garlic-chive aioli

Serves: **3**   Prep time: **15 minutes**   Cook time: **20 minutes**

• Dairy-free

"After having some delicious crab cakes over the holidays last year, I set out to make an equally tasty recipe for salmon cakes. These cakes are perfect for a party or just to spice up a weekly meal with something that seems a bit more 'fancy.' We top our salmon cakes with a squeeze of lemon juice and a dollop of delicious Garlic-Chive Aioli, but they are delicious on their own as well!"

1 (12-oz) can salmon, drained

3 large egg yolks

1/2 tsp sea salt

1 tsp ground black pepper

1/2 tsp paprika

1 clove garlic, smashed with the side of a knife and chopped (see Notes)

1/4 Vidalia onion, chopped (see Notes)

1 Tbsp duck fat or other cooking fat of choice

Garlic-Chive Aioli (pg 242)

Lemon wedges, for garnish

Preheat the oven to 350°F. Line a rimmed baking sheet with parchment paper.

In a large mixing bowl, combine the salmon, egg yolks, salt, pepper, and paprika. In a mini food processor, mince the garlic and onion. Add the minced garlic and onion to the salmon mixture and stir to combine the ingredients.

Using your hands, form the salmon mixture into 2-oz patties and place them on a clean plate. Heat the duck fat over medium-high heat in a well-seasoned cast-iron skillet. Once the fat is hot, turn the heat down to medium and fry the salmon cakes for about 1 minute per side, until browned and crispy.

Place the fried salmon cakes on the parchment-lined baking sheet and finish in the oven for 10–15 minutes. While the cakes are baking, prepare the Garlic-Chive Aioli. Serve the cakes topped with the aioli and a squeeze of lemon juice.

Cook's Notes:

Although they are going into the food processor, the garlic and onion need to be chopped into smaller pieces first so that you get uniform bits when you process them.

To make this recipe nut-free, use olive oil in place of the macadamia nut oil in the aioli.

santorini seafood stew

Serves: **4**   Prep time: **30 minutes**   Cook time: **30 minutes**

· Dairy-free   · Nut-free   · Egg-free

2 Tbsp ghee, store-bought or homemade (pg 286)

1/4 large Vidalia onion, chopped

4 large cloves garlic, smashed with the side of a knife

6 vine-ripened tomatoes, seeded and chopped

2 tsp tomato paste

1/4 tsp sea salt

10 grinds black pepper

1 bay leaf

1/2 tsp dried oregano

1/4 tsp red pepper flakes

1 head escarole, chopped

1 Tbsp capers

1 cup Chicken Stock (pg 278)

4 oz littleneck clams, rinsed under cold water (see Note)

4 oz mussels, rinsed under cold water (see Note)

8 oz large wild-caught shrimp, peeled and deveined, tails on

Melt the ghee in a soup pot over medium heat. Add the onion and garlic and sauté until the onion is translucent.

Add the tomatoes and tomato paste and sauté until the tomatoes soften and release some of their juices. Add the salt, pepper, bay leaf, oregano, and red pepper flakes and stir to combine.

Add the escarole and capers to the pot and stir to combine. Once the escarole has started to wilt, pour in the stock and stir to combine. Reduce the heat to medium-low and simmer, uncovered, for about 10 minutes to allow the flavors to come together.

Raise the heat to medium and add the clams to the pot. Cover and cook for 5 minutes. After 5 minutes, add the mussels. Allow the mussels and clams to cook until all of their shells have opened. Discard any that do not open after 10–15 minutes of cooking in the bubbling broth.

Transfer the clams and mussels to a large bowl. Add the shrimp to the pot and stir to make sure that all of the shrimp are mixed into the sauce. Cook until the shrimp are pink and opaque, about 2–3 minutes. Return the clams and mussels to the pot and stir to combine all of the shellfish with the sauce. Remove from the heat and serve.

Cook's Note:

If you're new to cooking shellfish (specifically bivalves like clams and mussels), here is a simple rule to follow to avoid bad clams or mussels: If it is open before cooking, do not cook it. If it does not open during cooking, do not eat it.

scallop ceviche

Serves: **2–4**   Prep time: **20 minutes**   Cook time: **2 hours**

• Dairy-free   • Nut-free   • Egg-free

8 oz sea scallops, diced

1/4 cup fresh orange juice

Juice of 1 lemon (3 Tbsp)

Juice of 1 lime (2 Tbsp)

1/2 jalapeño, seeded and finely diced

1/4 cup finely diced mango

2 Tbsp finely diced red onion

Sea salt and ground black pepper

1/2 tsp grated lemon zest

1 tsp chopped fresh cilantro leaves

Place the scallops and citrus juices in a nonreactive container and refrigerate until the scallops "cook" and turn opaque, approximately 2 hours.

Drain off the excess juice and combine the scallops with the remaining ingredients. Serve with grain-free chips or sliced vegetables, or eat the ceviche on its own!

Cook's Note:

You can enjoy this ceviche on its own or with organic corn chips (if tolerated) or taro chips.

shrimp, avocado, and grapefruit salad

Serves: **2**   Prep time: **15 minutes**   Cook time: **10 minutes**

• Nut-free   • Egg-free   • Nightshade-free

" One of my favorite ways to enjoy a salad is as a garnish of greens to accompany a flavorful protein. There is no need for lemon juice or vinegar in this salad: The grapefruit adds just the right amount of acidity. A simple drizzle of olive oil and a sprinkle of salt and pepper are all you need. "

2 Tbsp unsalted grass-fed butter

1 clove garlic, minced

10 large wild-caught shrimp, peeled and deveined, tails on

Sea salt and ground black pepper

1/4 tsp ground cardamom

4 cups mixed salad greens

1 grapefruit, segmented

1 avocado, peeled, pitted, and thinly sliced

Extra-virgin olive oil, for drizzling

Heat the butter in a skillet over medium heat. Add the garlic and sauté until fragrant, about 1 minute. Reduce the heat to medium-low and add the shrimp. Season with salt, pepper, and a sprinkle of cardamom. Flip the shrimp to cook the opposite side and season again with salt, pepper, and cardamom. Once the shrimp is no longer translucent (about 6 minutes total), remove it from the heat.

Divide the mixed salad greens between two plates and top with the grapefruit segments, avocado slices, a drizzle of olive oil, and a sprinkle of salt. Place the shrimp on top of the salad and serve.

Cook's Note:

To make this recipe dairy-free, use ghee or lard instead of butter.

shrimp and scallop scampi

Serves: **2**   Prep time: **35 minutes**   Cook time: **20 minutes**

• Nut-free   • Dairy-free   • Nightshade-free

"BUTTER" GARLIC SAUCE

3 Tbsp ghee, store-bought or homemade (pg 286)

5 cloves garlic, minced

Juice of 1/2 lemon (1 1/2 Tbsp)

1/2 cup Chicken Stock (pg 278)

1/2 tsp sea salt

6 grinds black pepper

Nut-Free Pasta Dough (pg 328)

1 Tbsp ghee, store-bought or homemade (pg 286)

6 oz sea scallops, rinsed under cold water and patted dry

8 oz wild-caught shrimp, peeled and deveined, tails on

Extra-virgin olive oil, for the pasta

2 Tbsp finely chopped fresh parsley, for garnish

Prepare the sauce: In a medium-sized saucepan, combine the 3 Tbsp of ghee with the garlic, lemon juice, stock, salt, and pepper. Bring to a simmer over medium-low heat and simmer for 5–10 minutes.

Prepare the pasta dough, but do not cook the noodles yet (complete the first three steps on pg 328). Bring a large pot of water to a boil while you prepare the rest of the ingredients.

Heat the 1 Tbsp of ghee in a skillet over medium heat. Sauté the scallops until they get a nice golden sear on each side, 6–8 minutes total. Remove the seared scallops and set aside. Add the shrimp to the hot pan and cook until they are pink and opaque. Return the scallops to the pan, reduce the heat to medium-low, and add about half of the sauce. Keep warm over low heat.

Once the pot of water is gently boiling, carefully add the noodles and boil for approximately 3 minutes. Rinse under cold water and gently toss with a drizzle of olive oil to prevent the noodles from sticking to one another.

Toss the shrimp and scallops in the remaining sauce and pour over the noodles. Garnish with the parsley and serve.

smoked flounder hand rolls

Yield: **6 hand rolls**   Prep time: **25 minutes**   Cook time: **1 1/2 hours**

· Dairy-free   · Nut-free   · Nightshade-free

 "You can put pretty much anything in a hand roll and I will devour it. Hand rolls are great for beginners who have never worked with nori (seaweed) before. When making hand rolls, be aware that as soon as the nori touches any type of moisture, it is going to lose its shape within minutes. If the hand roll is completed quickly, it will maintain its shape well enough on the plate, but the longer you take to roll it, the more difficult it will become to handle. "

1 (12-oz) flounder fillet

1/4 tsp sea salt

1/8 tsp ground black pepper

1/8 tsp ground dried lemon peel

3 sheets nori

1 cucumber, julienned

Lemon-Caper Aioli (pg 246)

Special equipment:

Cedar plank

Smoker

Rinse and pat dry the flounder. Place the fish on the cedar plank and sprinkle with the salt, pepper, and lemon peel. Place in the smoker on a low setting (220°F) for 90 minutes, or until the flounder has a golden color and flakes easily.

Allow the fish to cool, roughly 15 minutes. Using a fork, gently shred the smoked flounder.

Cut the sheets of nori in half by placing your knife blade along the center of the sheet and firmly pressing down. Do not drag the knife to cut the nori, as this will tear the sheet. Place some flounder, cucumber, and aioli on half of a nori sheet. Roll the nori to create a cone shape, and wrap the excess nori around the back of the hand roll. Repeat with the remaining nori, flounder, cucumber, and aioli.

Cook's Note:

You can also make this recipe on the grill. Soak the cedar plank for 2 hours prior to beginning. Grill the fish over low heat for 15-20 minutes, and monitor to make sure that the plank does not burn.

spicy tuna dip

Serves: **2–4**   Time needed: **10 minutes**

· Dairy-free   · Nut-free

 66Spicy tuna is one of the most popular sushi items eaten in the United States. I wanted to put a spin on this favorite and create a wonderful dish that can be shared with others. This dip is ultrafresh and goes well with sliced vegetables or small pieces of nori. The key to finding sushi-grade tuna where you live is talking to the fishmonger at your market. Most stores will reserve sushi-grade fish for customers, but you have to ask. Another place to check is a Japanese grocery store if you're lucky enough to have one near you. We have one nearby, and fresh fish is delivered to it three times a week. Use the fish the same day you purchase it, as changes in refrigerator temperature will disrupt the flavor. 99

4 oz sushi-grade tuna

1 Tbsp Chipotle Habanero Pepper Sauce (see Note)

1 tsp raw honey

1 tsp apple cider vinegar

1/4 tsp toasted sesame oil

1 Tbsp katsuobushi

1/4 tsp sea salt

1 Tbsp mayonnaise, store-bought or homemade (pg 244)

1 Tbsp thinly sliced scallion, plus more for garnish

1 tsp toasted sesame seeds

1 tsp coconut aminos

Cucumber slices, for serving

Avocado slices, for serving

Take a spoon and, with a scraping motion, gently separate the flesh of the tuna from the connective tissues. Place the scraped tuna in a medium-sized mixing bowl and set aside. If some connective tissue makes it into the dip, it will not harm you or greatly affect the flavor of the dip, but a lot of connective tissue can impact the texture.

In a small bowl, whisk the pepper sauce, honey, and vinegar until blended.

Using a fork, gently incorporate the remaining ingredients. Serve with sliced cucumber and avocado, garnished with scallions.

Cook's Note:

We use Organic Harvest Foods' Chipotle Habanero Pepper Sauce. If you can't find this brand, you can substitute your favorite smoky hot pepper sauce.

whole roasted mackerel

Serves: **2**   Prep time: **20 minutes**   Cook time: **25 minutes**

· Dairy-free   · Nut-free   · Egg-free   · Nightshade-free

1 (1-lb) whole mackerel (see Notes)

2 scallions

1/2 lemon, thinly sliced (5 slices)

4 cloves garlic, smashed with the side of a knife

1/2 cup kosher salt

2 Tbsp grated fresh ginger

1 Tbsp extra-virgin olive oil

Basic Cauliflower Rice (pg 188; optional)

Preheat the oven to 450°F.

Rinse the fish cavity to remove any remaining blood. Pat dry with a paper towel. Stuff the cavity with the scallions, 2 slices of lemon, and garlic. Using cooking twine, tie the fish to secure the ingredients inside the cavity.

In a small mixing bowl, combine the salt and ginger and mix thoroughly. Place the fish on a rimmed baking sheet. Drizzle the olive oil over the fish, then use your hands to rub the oil over the fish to coat it evenly. Rub the salt and ginger mixture over the skin, coating the fish evenly. Arrange the remaining 3 lemon slices on top of the fish.

Roast the fish for 20–25 minutes, until the internal temperature reaches 145°F (see Notes). Serve with cauliflower rice, if desired.

Cook's Notes:

When you purchase your whole mackerel, ask the fishmonger to gut the fish and remove the gills.

It's best to cook this dish with a meat thermometer nearby. When you're dealing with a fish as oily as mackerel, there are always going to be slight variations in cooking time. As with all meat, you should check the temperature in the thickest part of the fish, between the spine and the pectoral fin.

If you're not a fan of mackerel, this recipe would work well with most whole white fish.

plants

apple bacon butternut squash soup

Serves: **4**   Prep time: **45 minutes**   Cook time: **15 minutes**

· Nut-free   · Egg-free   · Nightshade-free

3 Tbsp unsalted grass-fed butter

1 medium butternut squash, peeled and cubed

1/2 medium yellow onion, chopped

3 cloves garlic, minced

7 strips bacon, chopped (reserve 2 for garnish)

2 Granny Smith apples

3 cups Chicken Stock (pg 278)

1/2 tsp ground dried sage

1 tsp ground cinnamon

Sea salt and ground black pepper

Extra-virgin olive oil, for drizzling

Preheat the oven to 425°F. Grease a rimmed baking sheet with the butter.

Place the squash on the prepared baking sheet and roast for 40 minutes, until the flesh is fork-tender and the edges are golden.

In a soup pot over medium-low heat, combine the onion, garlic, and 5 strips of the chopped bacon. Cook until the onion softens and the bacon crisps, stirring frequently, approximately 7–10 minutes.

Peel and dice the apples and add them to the soup pot. Continue to cook for an additional 10 minutes, stirring often. Add the roasted squash, stock, sage, cinnamon, salt, and pepper to the pot. Bring the soup to a low boil, then reduce the heat to low and simmer for 15 minutes.

In a small frying pan, fry the remaining chopped bacon until crispy.

Purée the soup with an immersion blender or high-speed blender until smooth and creamy.

Serve the soup topped with the crispy bacon and a drizzle of olive oil.

Cook's Note:

To make this recipe dairy-free, use ghee or lard instead of butter.

baby broccoli with bacon

Serves: **4**   Prep time: **5 minutes**   Cook time: **30 minutes**

· Dairy-free   · Nut-free   · Egg-free   · Nightshade-free

2 strips bacon, chopped

1 lb baby broccoli (see Note)

Sea salt and ground black pepper

2 cloves garlic, pressed

Up to 3 Tbsp bacon fat or ghee, store-bought or homemade (pg 286)

Preheat the oven to 400°F.

Sauté the bacon in a large cast-iron skillet or other ovenproof skillet over medium heat until crispy. Remove the bacon from the skillet and set aside, leaving the rendered bacon fat in the pan.

Add the baby broccoli to the skillet and sauté over medium heat until softened, about 5 minutes. Season with salt and pepper and add up to 3 Tbsp more bacon fat if needed to keep the broccoli from sticking to the pan.

Once the broccoli has softened, place the skillet in the oven to roast for 10 minutes. After 10 minutes, add the pressed garlic and roast for another 5 minutes.

Remove the broccoli from the oven and sprinkle with the chopped bacon before serving.

Cook's Note:

Baby broccoli is also known as broccolini. It is not to be confused with broccoli rabe, which is extremely bitter. Baby broccoli has a flavor similar to regular broccoli, but has smaller florets and longer, thinner stalks. If you can't find baby broccoli near you, regular broccoli will work just fine in this recipe.

bacon and yellow squash hash

Serves: **2**   Prep time: **10 minutes**   Cook time: **20 minutes**

• Dairy-free   • Nut-free   • Nightshade-free

 66 This recipe is based on a comforting breakfast dish that an old roommate, Sarah Jane, used to make for me. After I moved back to the United States from the Dominican Republic and was doing my fair share of couch surfing, this dish became a regular morning meal for me. It features yellow squash, a vegetable that, though common in the States, was completely missing from my diet while I was living in the D.R. I craved it, along with other hard-to-find vegetables, constantly. Sometimes topped with melted cheese, this dish is easy and delicious—perfectly comforting for end-of-winter mornings. 99

3 strips bacon, diced

1/4 yellow onion, diced

3 yellow squash, sliced

1 1/2 tsp ground cinnamon

1 tsp garlic powder

1/2 tsp dried rosemary

1 Tbsp ghee, store-bought or homemade (pg 286)

2 large eggs

2 scallions, thinly sliced, for garnish

In a medium-sized skillet over medium heat, cook the bacon until it has released enough fat to sauté the other ingredients, about 6 minutes. Add the onion and continue sautéing until the onion is translucent and the bacon is beginning to crisp. Add the squash, cinnamon, garlic powder, and rosemary and sauté until the squash is soft and lightly browned around the edges.

In a separate skillet, heat the ghee over medium-low heat. Fry 2 eggs to your liking and place them over the top of the hash.

Garnish with the scallions and serve.

basic cauliflower rice

Serves: **4**   Prep time: **10 minutes**   Cook time: **10 minutes**

· Dairy-free   · Nut-free   · Egg-free   · Nightshade-free

❝ Basic Cauliflower Rice is a very simple recipe, and it is the perfect grain-free alternative to rice. It's a fantastic base for curry, stew, or any slow-cooked meat and vegetable dish that is typically served over rice. ❞

1 head cauliflower (about 1 1/2 lbs)

1 Tbsp ghee, store-bought or homemade (pg 286)

1/2 tsp sea salt

1/4 tsp ground black pepper

Chopped fresh parsley, for garnish (optional)

Chop the cauliflower into large florets. Using the side of a box grater with the largest holes, grate the cauliflower into "rice."

Warm the ghee in a large skillet over medium heat. Add the grated cauliflower and season with the salt and pepper. Sauté, uncovered, until just tender, about 5 minutes.

Garnish with fresh parsley, if desired, and serve.

Cook's Note:

Be sure to not overcook your cauliflower, as overcooking will make it too soft and mushy. Cook it only until tender so that it has a texture similar to rice.

beet and goat cheese salad

Serves: **4**   Prep time: **20 minutes**   Cook time: **1 hour**

• Egg-free

 66 On our honeymoon last year, Hayley and I enjoyed exploring Puerto Vallarta and its many fabulous restaurants. There was one restaurant in particular that we visited twice during the week, and both times we ordered the dish that inspired this recipe. This salad is full of great flavors and textures and will always hold a special place in our hearts as a reminder of our honeymoon. 99

SALAD

2 medium golden beets

2 medium purple beets

2 Tbsp coconut oil, divided

6 cups arugula

1/4 cup crumbled goat cheese

1/2 cup sliced cherry tomatoes

1/4 cup chopped roasted and salted pistachio meats

STRAWBERRY BALSAMIC REDUCTION

12 strawberries, sliced

3/4 cup balsamic vinegar

2 Tbsp raw honey

1 Tbsp plus 1 tsp fresh lemon juice

1 Tbsp filtered water

Roast the beets: Preheat the oven to 375°F. Rinse the beets and cut off the stem and tip ends. Lay out two sheets of foil, each large enough to wrap up two beets. Place the two golden beets on one sheet of foil and the two purple beets on the other. Before enclosing, place 1 1/2 tsp of the coconut oil on each of the beets. Enclose the beets in the foil so that they will steam. Place the beets in the oven for approximately 1 hour, until fork-tender, then remove from the oven and allow to cool.

Meanwhile, make the reduction: Combine the strawberries, balsamic vinegar, honey, lemon juice, and water in a small saucepan. Bring to a boil, then reduce the heat to low. Once the strawberries have softened, pulverize them in the saucepan. Cook the mixture until reduced to the desired thickness, about 8–10 minutes. Remove from the heat and strain the liquid.

Peel the cooled beets. The skin should peel away easily. Slice into 1/2-inch-thick slices.

To serve, divide the arugula among four plates. Arrange the beet slices on top, alternating the colors, then top with the goat cheese, tomatoes, pistachios, and Strawberry Balsamic Reduction.

braised brussels sprouts

Serves: **4**   Prep time: **20 minutes**   Cook time: **1 hour**

· Dairy-free   · Nut-free   · Egg-free   · Nightshade-free

❝Our typical preparation for Brussels sprouts is to roast them in the oven. However, we sometimes like to change things up with this dish, in which they are gently braised in a savory stock with coconut aminos. The result is a hearty side that pairs well with any protein.❞

1 1/2 Tbsp ghee, store-bought or homemade (pg 286), divided

1 shallot, thinly sliced

2 large cloves garlic, chopped

1 1/2 lbs Brussels sprouts (about 3 cups), sliced in half or quartered if large

Sea salt and ground black pepper

2 Tbsp coconut aminos

1 cup Chicken Stock (pg 278)

Heat 1 Tbsp of the ghee in a 3-quart sauté pan over medium heat. Add the shallot and garlic and sauté until fragrant, about 5 minutes, reducing the heat to medium-low if the shallot or garlic seems like it may start to burn.

Add the Brussels sprouts, season with salt and pepper, add the remaining 1/2 Tbsp of ghee, and sauté until the Brussels sprouts start to soften slightly and brown a bit, 5–10 minutes. Add the coconut aminos and stir to evenly combine.

Pour the stock over the Brussels sprouts and stir to combine. Reduce the heat to low, cover, and cook for at least 1 hour, until they are soft.

caramelized carrots

Serves: **3**   Prep time: **10 minutes**   Cook time: **20 minutes**

· Nut-free   · Egg-free   · Nightshade-free

6 medium carrots, peeled

3 Tbsp unsalted grass-fed butter

1/4 cup coconut aminos

1/4 cup filtered water

Sea salt and ground black pepper

Chopped fresh parsley, for garnish

Place the carrots in a large skillet. Cut each tablespoon of butter in half and place three pats on top of the carrots and three pats in the bottom of the skillet around the carrots.

Pour the coconut aminos and water evenly over the carrots and season with a pinch of salt and pepper.

Set the skillet over medium heat and cover with a lid. Cook for 12 minutes, then remove the lid and roll the carrots around in the liquid to make sure that they are evenly coated. Reduce the heat to medium-low and continue cooking until the carrots are fork-tender, about 8 minutes.

Spoon any remaining liquid over the carrots and turn the carrots again to coat them in the sauce before serving. Garnish with cracked black pepper and chopped fresh parsley.

caramelized fennel with sweet potato puree

Serves: **4**   Prep time: **10 minutes**   Cook time: **30 minutes**

· Nut-free   · Egg-free   · Nightshade-free

 " Fennel is arguably an underrated and underutilized ingredient in Western cuisine. This plant is a member of the celery family, though it tastes nothing like celery. With a flavor note of anise, it can add a unique taste and texture to summertime dishes. While the textural counterpoint in this dish is really fun, the flavors are the true star of the show. "

2 medium sweet potatoes, peeled and chopped

2 Tbsp pure maple syrup

1 1/2 fennel bulbs (1 1/2 lbs; reserve fronds for garnish, if desired)

3 Tbsp unsalted grass-fed butter, divided

1/2 tsp sea salt

7 grinds black pepper

1/2 tsp ground cardamom

Preheat the oven to 400°F.

In a glass baking dish, combine the sweet potatoes and maple syrup. Bake for 20 minutes, until you can easily pierce them with a fork. While the sweet potatoes are baking, prepare the fennel bulbs.

Slice the fennel bulbs to 1/2-inch thickness. Heat 1 1/2 Tbsp of the butter in a skillet over medium heat. Add the fennel and cook until golden brown and caramelized, about 15–20 minutes.

Place the cooked sweet potatoes in a food processor along with the salt, pepper, cardamom, and remaining 1 1/2 Tbsp of butter and process until smooth.

Serve the sweet potato puree topped with the caramelized fennel and garnished with a sprinkling of chopped fennel fronds, if desired.

Cook's Note:

To make this recipe dairy-free, use ghee or lard instead of butter.

cauliflower couscous

Serves: **4**   Prep time: **15 minutes**   Cook time: **25 minutes**

· Dairy-free   · Egg-free

 " This is another Staley family favorite, reinterpreted with Paleo-friendly ingredients. The major swap in this dish is replacing couscous with riced cauliflower. The trick to getting the correct texture from the cauliflower is all in the shredding technique. This summer side dish is the perfect way to utilize fresh ingredients and enjoy something that's very light on the palate. "

1/3 cup pine nuts

2 cloves garlic, pressed

2 Tbsp duck fat, divided

2 medium carrots, peeled and sliced

1 yellow bell pepper, diced

1 cup sliced cherry tomatoes

1 tsp sea salt

25 grinds black pepper

1/2 large head cauliflower

4 scallions, sliced

GARNISHES

Lemon wedges

Extra-virgin olive oil

Fresh flat-leaf parsley, roughly chopped

In a large skillet over medium heat, sauté the pine nuts and garlic in 1 Tbsp of the duck fat. When the pine nuts are golden brown, remove them from the skillet and set aside. Add the remaining 1 Tbsp of duck fat to the skillet and sauté the carrots, bell pepper, and tomatoes for about 15 minutes, until soft. Season with the salt and pepper.

Grate the cauliflower with the stems parallel to the grating surface (giving you longer grains of "rice"). Add the cauliflower to the skillet along with the sliced scallions, toasted pine nuts, and garlic.

Serve with a squeeze of lemon juice and a drizzle of olive oil, garnished with flat-leaf parsley.

Cook's Note:

To make this recipe nut-free, simply omit the pine nuts.

celery root puree

Serves: **8**   Prep time: **15 minutes**   Cook time: **30 minutes**

· Nut-free   · Egg-free   · Nightshade-free

2 celery root bulbs

2 large white carrots (see Notes)

4 cups Chicken Stock (pg 278)

2 cups filtered water

3 Tbsp unsalted grass-fed butter

1 tsp sea salt

1 tsp ground black pepper

1/2 tsp garlic powder

1/2 tsp onion powder

1/4 tsp rubbed sage

Extra-virgin olive oil, for drizzling

Rinse and peel the celery root and carrots. Chop them into large chunks and place them in a soup pot. Cover the vegetables with the stock and water. Turn on the heat to medium and cook the vegetables for about 30 minutes, until they are fork-tender.

Drain the vegetables and place them in a high-speed blender or food processor. Add the butter and purée until smooth. Add the salt, pepper, garlic powder, onion powder, and sage and purée again until the mixture is whipped and fluffy.

To serve, plate the puree, drizzle with olive oil, and season with cracked black pepper, if desired.

Cook's Notes:

White carrots are easily found in late summer and fall, which is their harvest season. You can substitute parsnips to preserve the white color of the puree, or you can use orange carrots if you don't mind the change in color.

This recipe makes a big batch. It's helpful to add the vegetables to the blender or food processor a little at a time.

To make this recipe dairy-free, use ghee or lard instead of butter.

cold sesame zoodles

Serves: **2–4**   Prep time: **20 minutes**   Cook time: **25 minutes**

· Dairy-free   · Nut-free   · Egg-free

❝I am a sucker for cold noodles. Not only are they typically delicious, but they can be put away and lazily eaten directly out of the fridge without sacrificing the deliciousness of a dish eaten at its appropriate temperature. Zucchini noodles are perfect for this dish, though they do not have as long a shelf life as rice noodles and become soggy more quickly. I suggest eating this cold dish within a couple days. ❞

SESAME SAUCE

1/4 cup plus 2 Tbsp tahini

1/2 cup filtered water

1/2 tsp fish sauce

2 cloves garlic, minced

1/2 tsp grated fresh ginger

1 tsp toasted sesame oil

1/4 cup plus 2 Tbsp coconut aminos

1 1/2 tsp coconut sugar

1 1/2 tsp white wine vinegar

3/4 tsp red pepper flakes

1 medium zucchini

2 medium carrots, peeled

Toasted sesame seeds, for garnish

Fresh cilantro leaves, for garnish

Make the sesame sauce: In a medium-sized saucepan, whisk together all of the ingredients for the sauce until blended. Cook over medium-low heat until the sauce thickens slightly, whisking occasionally, approximately 7 minutes. Remove from the heat and allow to cool completely.

Make the "noodles": Chop off the ends of the zucchini. Use a spiral slicer to create long, curly noodles according to the manufacturer's instructions. Cut off the ends of the carrots and julienne them using a julienne peeler, making the cuts the length of the carrots. Place the zoodles and julienned carrots in a steamer basket set over a pot of boiling water and steam for 15 minutes. Pour the steamed zoodles and carrots into a colander and rinse under cold water. Allow the water to drain completely before tossing the noodles with the sauce.

Combine the cooled noodles with the sesame sauce and serve garnished with toasted sesame seeds and cilantro.

ethiopian cabbage

Serves: **8**   Prep time: **20 minutes**   Cook time: **1 hour**

· Dairy-free   · Nut-free   · Egg-free   · Nightshade-free

66 Hayley and I fell in love with this dish during our visit to Portland last year while traveling with Diane Sanfilippo for a book tour. Portland might have been our favorite stop on the tour because we got to eat several meals from the Cultured Caveman food carts. Heather and Joe, the owners, have an Ethiopian cabbage dish on the menu, which we loved! If you ever have the chance to dine with them, do yourself a favor and order it. Until then, you can make our version of this tasty side dish. 99

1 Tbsp duck fat

1 1/2 cups chopped Vidalia onion

1 head green cabbage, thinly sliced

Sea salt and ground black pepper

3 carrots, peeled and grated

1 1/4 tsp garlic powder

1 1/4 tsp ground ginger

1 tsp ground turmeric

Heat the duck fat in a large sauté pan over medium heat. Add the onion and sauté until translucent.

Add the cabbage and continue to sauté until the cabbage starts to soften, about 10 minutes. Season with salt and pepper.

Add the carrots and stir to combine with the cabbage. Add the garlic powder, ginger, and turmeric and stir to incorporate the spices evenly into the cabbage.

Reduce the heat to low and cover the pan. Cook for 1 hour, stirring every so often.

home fries

Serves: **4**   Prep time: **10 minutes**   Cook time: **35 minutes**

· Dairy-free   · Nut-free   · Egg-free

66 Everyone has their own way of making home fries, and this happens to be ours. Like many of the dishes in this book, this is one that we brought back from our travels. We enjoyed it at a small café in Sayulita during our honeymoon. The spice blend is what really makes this dish shine. We love whipping up a big batch of these home fries for family when we get together for brunch—it's a crowd-pleaser! Serve with eggs cooked to your liking and Pico de Gallo (pg 254). 99

3-4 medium russet potatoes (1 1/2 lbs)

2 Tbsp duck fat or Rendered Lard (pg 294)

1 tsp paprika

1 tsp onion powder

1 tsp garlic powder

1 tsp dried oregano

1 tsp sea salt

1/2 tsp ground black pepper

Peel and rinse the potatoes. Cut them into 1/2-inch cubes and set aside.

Preheat the oven to 400°F.

Heat the duck fat in an ovenproof skillet (preferably cast iron) over medium heat. Add the potatoes and set a timer for 10 minutes, stirring every minute to make sure that they do not stick to the pan. Meanwhile, mix together the spices and salt.

After sautéing the potatoes for 10 minutes, dust them as evenly as possible with the spice blend. Sauté for an additional 5 minutes, continuing to stir every minute and adding additional duck fat as necessary to prevent the potatoes from sticking.

Transfer the skillet to the oven and bake for 15 minutes. While the potatoes are baking, prepare any dishes you'd like to serve with the potatoes. After 15 minutes, stir the potatoes, then return them to the oven and cook for a final 5 minutes, until golden brown and delicious.

Cook's Note:

Although home fries are great made with classic russet potatoes, we really enjoy making this dish with sweet potatoes as well. The sweetness of sweet potatoes pairs nicely with the spice blend.

mango and avocado salad

Serves: **4**   Time needed: **10 minutes**

· Dairy-free   · Nut-free   · Egg-free

“ This refreshing salad is perfect for spring or summer. For a complete meal, pair it with grilled fish or chicken, either with the salad on the side or with the protein on top! ”

2 cups mixed salad greens

1 cup baby arugula

1/2 mango, peeled and sliced

1/2 avocado, peeled, pitted, and sliced

1/2 shallot, thinly sliced

2 Tbsp chopped fresh cilantro

Citrus Vinaigrette (pg 238)

Combine the mixed salad greens with the baby arugula on a salad platter.

Arrange the mango and avocado slices over the greens and sprinkle with the shallot and cilantro.

Dress the salad with the vinaigrette and serve.

Cook's Note:

To make this recipe nightshade-free, omit the red pepper flakes from the Citrus Vinaigrette.

minestrone

Serves: **6**   Prep time: **30 minutes**   Cook time: **2–3 hours**

· Nut-free   · Egg-free

1 Tbsp unsalted grass-fed butter

1/2 large Vidalia onion, diced

3 cloves garlic, smashed with the side of a knife and chopped

2 large carrots, peeled and chopped

2 celery stalks, sliced

1 1/4 tsp sea salt, divided

Ground black pepper

4 large Roma tomatoes, seeded and diced, divided

1 tsp dried oregano

1 tsp dried basil

7 cups Chicken Stock (pg 278)

1/2 lb green beans, trimmed and cut into 1-inch sections

In a large soup pot over medium heat, melt the butter. Sauté the onion and garlic until the onion is soft and translucent, about 7 minutes. Add the carrots and celery and continue to sauté for a few moments, until they start to glisten.

Season the vegetables with 1 tsp of the salt and a few grinds of pepper. Reduce the heat to medium-low and continue to cook until the vegetables have softened, about 10 minutes.

While the vegetables are cooking, pulse half of the diced tomatoes in a food processor until they are crushed. Place the crushed tomatoes and remaining diced tomatoes in the soup pot and stir to combine with the other vegetables.

Add the oregano and basil to the pot and stir to combine. Pour the stock over the vegetables. Add the green beans and stir to combine all of the vegetables with the stock.

Increase the heat to medium-high and bring the soup to a boil. Once the soup has come to a boil, reduce the heat and simmer, stirring occasionally, for up to 3 hours to allow the flavors to really develop. After the soup has cooked for just over an hour, taste it, and add salt if needed to enhance the flavor.

Cook's Notes:

If you use store-bought chicken broth instead of homemade stock, opt for low-sodium broth and taste the soup after it has cooked for a bit before salting.

To make this recipe dairy-free, use ghee or lard instead of butter.

oven-roasted summer vegetables with herbs

Serves: **4**   Prep time: **10 minutes**   Cook time: **35 minutes**

· Dairy-free   · Nut-free   · Egg-free

"A dish that is as gorgeous as it is delicious, these simple roasted vegetables are just what we need to get us excited for summertime cooking. Full of color and flavor, this elegant side dish can be made quickly for any summer fling."

1 small eggplant

2 yellow squash

1 medium zucchini

6 Brussels sprouts

2 small or 1 large Vidalia salad onion

2 Tbsp coconut oil, melted

1 tsp dried oregano

1 tsp sea salt

1 tsp ground black pepper

Preheat the oven to 350°F.

Slice all of the vegetables to 1/4-inch thickness and lightly toss with the melted coconut oil. Arrange the vegetables on a large baking sheet lined with parchment paper and roast for 20 minutes.

Remove the vegetables from the oven and season with the oregano, salt, and pepper. If it looks like the vegetables are starting to brown too quickly (or burn), cover with foil. Return the vegetables to the oven for a final 15 minutes, or until tender.

Cook's Note:

This dish can be made at different times of the year using seasonal vegetables. In the spring, we like to use Vidalia spring (or "baby") onions, which not only taste delicious but are visually beautiful as well.

poached pear salad with crispy shallots and caramelized maple balsamic

Serves: **4**   Prep time: **15 minutes**   Cook time: **30 minutes**

· Nut-free   · Egg-free   · Nightshade-free

Caramelized Maple Balsamic (pg 234)

4 cups filtered water

2 cups cherry juice (no sugar added)

1 Tbsp grated fresh ginger

1 pear, thinly sliced

Duck fat or other cooking fat of choice, for frying

1 medium shallot, thinly sliced

4 cups baby greens

Mild bleu cheese, for garnish (optional; omit for dairy-free)

Prepare the Caramelized Maple Balsamic.

Combine the water, cherry juice, and ginger in a medium-sized saucepan and bring to a simmer over medium heat. Add the pear slices and poach until soft, about 7 minutes. Drain the pear slices and set aside to cool.

In a separate small saucepan, warm about 3/4 inch of duck fat over medium-low heat. Test the temperature of the fat with one piece of shallot before adding more. When the oil is hot, add the sliced shallots in batches so as not to overcrowd the pan and gently deep-fry until golden and crispy, about 2 minutes per batch. Using a slotted spoon, remove the shallots to paper towels to drain.

To serve, divide the greens and pears among four plates. Dress the salad with the Caramelized Maple Balsamic and top with the crispy shallots and crumbled bleu cheese, if desired.

roasted head of cauliflower

Serves: **6**   Prep time: **15 minutes**   Cook time: **1 hour**

· Dairy-free   · Nut-free   · Egg-free   · Nightshade-free

1 head cauliflower (about 1 1/2 lbs), stem and leaves removed

3 Tbsp ghee, store-bought or homemade (pg 286)

3/4 tsp sea salt

2 cloves garlic, minced

Grated zest of 1 small lemon

Juice of 1/2 small lemon (1 Tbsp)

1 tsp minced fresh thyme leaves

1/2 cup Chicken Stock (pg 278)

5 grinds black pepper

Preheat the oven to 375°F.

Rinse the cauliflower under cold water and pat dry. Place it in a rimmed baking dish. Melt the ghee in a small saucepan over low heat. Pour the melted ghee over the cauliflower and season with the salt. Place in the oven and roast for 30 minutes. (Do not clean the saucepan; you will use it in the next step.)

While the cauliflower is roasting, place the garlic, lemon zest, lemon juice, thyme, and stock in the same small saucepan. Whisk to combine and warm the mixture over low heat, just to allow the flavors to meld.

After the cauliflower has roasted for 30 minutes, pour the sauce over the cauliflower, season with the pepper, and roast for an additional 30 minutes, or until the cauliflower is nicely browned on top and fork-tender in the middle.

Cook's Note:

If the cauliflower is becoming too brown on top before it has finished cooking, tent it with foil to avoid overcooking the outside.

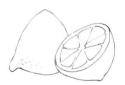

roasted potatoes, carrots, and celery

Serves: **6**   Prep time: **20 minutes**   Cook time: **35–40 minutes**

· Dairy-free   · Nut-free   · Egg-free

 66 This dish is a great option for any holiday meal or gathering. It is the perfect accompaniment to our Roasted Cornish Game Hens (pg 134), as shown together on the cover of this book. 99

1 1/2-2 lbs multicolored fingerling potatoes

3 stalks celery

2 large carrots, peeled

3 Tbsp duck fat, melted, divided

1 red onion, chopped (see Note)

2 heads garlic, quartered (see Note)

1 lemon, thinly sliced

2 tsp dried oregano

Sea salt and ground black pepper

Preheat the oven to 375°F.

Slice the potatoes in half lengthwise, and quarter the larger ones. Slice the celery and carrots on the diagonal. Place the potatoes, celery, and carrots in a large mixing bowl. Drizzle 2 Tbsp of the melted duck fat over them and stir to coat.

Pour the vegetables onto a rimmed baking sheet. Add the red onion, garlic, and lemon slices and drizzle the remaining 1 Tbsp of melted duck fat over the top to coat the onion, garlic, and lemon. Season with the oregano and a liberal amount of salt and pepper.

Roast for 35–40 minutes, until the outsides of the vegetables are browned and the insides are soft. After 20 minutes, test a potato with a fork to see if it's tender and to make sure that the vegetables are cooking evenly. Stir if needed.

Cook's Note:

For the purpose of presentation, we prefer to leave the onion in larger pieces and the garlic unpeeled and just tuck them into the tray of vegetables to roast as aromatics. For practicality, you can chop the onion into bite-sized pieces and quarter the garlic heads to roast, as directed above. This dish is beautiful either way.

roasted sweet potatoes with citrus dressing

Serves: **6**   Prep time: **20 minutes**   Cook time: **40 minutes**

· Dairy-free   · Nut-free   · Egg-free   · Nightshade-free

3 large white sweet potatoes

1 1/2 Tbsp coconut oil, melted

1 tsp sea salt

Grated zest of 1/2 lemon

CITRUS DRESSING

Juice of 1 lemon (3 Tbsp)

1/4 cup extra-virgin olive oil

2 Tbsp filtered water

Pinch of sea salt and ground black pepper

2 tsp coconut sugar

1/4 cup (a handful) fresh cilantro leaves, chopped

1 Tbsp chopped fresh chives

1/4 medium shallot, thinly sliced

Preheat the oven to 375°F.

Peel and chop the sweet potatoes into bite-sized pieces. Spread the sweet potato pieces evenly over a large rimmed baking sheet lightly greased with coconut oil. Toss with the melted coconut oil and season with the salt. Roast for 40 minutes, or until fork-tender, stirring every 15 minutes to ensure that they cook evenly and to prevent burning.

While the sweet potatoes are roasting, make the dressing: Combine the lemon juice, olive oil, water, salt, and pepper in a small mixing bowl, whisking to blend the oil with the acid. Add the coconut sugar and whisk again until it has dissolved into the dressing. Add the cilantro, chives, and shallot and whisk again to combine all of the ingredients.

Remove the sweet potatoes from the oven and carefully transfer them to a large glass mixing bowl. Pour the dressing over the potatoes and carefully mix to coat the potatoes evenly in the dressing. Sprinkle the lemon zest over top of the potatoes and stir again. This dish can be served warm or cold.

smoky slaw

Serves: **4**   Time needed: **25 minutes**

· Dairy-free   · Nut-free

❝A summertime cookout just isn't complete without a creamy coleslaw. This side dish goes really well with Fish Tacos (pg 154) or a big slab of Smoked Ribs (pg 106). The chipotle powder spices up this recipe without giving it too much of a kick, though you're welcome to add more if piquancy is something you crave! The smokiness of this slaw is perfectly balanced by the crunchy veggies and the creamy mayonnaise. ❞

3/4 cup Homemade Mayonnaise (pg 244)

1/2 medium green cabbage, thinly sliced

2 carrots, peeled and julienned

1/4 red onion, finely diced

1/2 tsp chipotle powder

1/2 tsp sea salt

10 grinds black pepper

Juice of 1/2 lime (1 Tbsp)

Prepare the Homemade Mayonnaise.

Place the cabbage, carrots, and red onion in a large mixing bowl.

Make the dressing: In a small mixing bowl, whisk together the mayonnaise, chipotle powder, salt, pepper, and lime juice.

Pour the dressing over the vegetables and toss to coat. The slaw will keep in the refrigerator for up to 3–5 days.

spiced cranberry relish

Serves: **8**   Prep time: **10 minutes**   Cook time: **25 minutes**

· Dairy-free   · Nut-free   · Egg-free   · Nightshade-free

1 (12-oz) bag fresh cranberries, preferably organic

Grated zest and juice of 1 orange

1 cup filtered water

1/2 cup granulated maple sugar

1 tsp pure vanilla extract

1/4 tsp ground allspice

1 Tbsp arrowroot starch (optional)

Rinse the cranberries under cold water and place them in a medium-sized saucepan. Add the orange zest, orange juice, and water and turn on the burner to medium heat. Cook, stirring, until the cranberries start to pop and bubble, about 3–5 minutes. Reduce the heat to medium-low and continue to cook, stirring often, until you have a mixture of softened, almost gelled cranberries and some that are still whole.

Stir in the maple sugar, vanilla extract, and allspice and cook for another 5 minutes or so, then reduce the heat to low.

If you want a thicker sauce, you can either allow the sauce to continue to reduce over low heat, stirring frequently, or add the arrowroot starch. Typically you want to add starch to a cool liquid or whisk it vigorously into a hot liquid so that it dissolves properly, but that's not possible with this relish, so just stir vigorously and the starch will dissolve just fine.

Remove the relish from the heat and serve immediately, or allow to cool if using as the filling for Cranberry Hand Pies (pg 360). If you are making this recipe for a holiday or family gathering, you can prepare it a day or two in advance and keep it in a sealed container in the fridge.

Cook's Note:

This recipe makes more relish than needed for the Cranberry Hand Pies, so you can serve the remainder at your holiday dinner or use it to make another batch of the hand pies.

stuffed acorn squash

Serves: **4**   Prep time: **30 minutes**   Cook time: **45 minutes**

· Dairy-free   · Nut-free   · Egg-free   · Nightshade-free

2 acorn squash

Up to 2 1/2 Tbsp ghee,
store-bought or homemade
(pg 286)

Sea salt

1 lb ground pork

3 medium carrots, peeled
and diced

5 white mushrooms, diced

1/2 Vidalia onion, diced

Ground black pepper

1 tsp fresh thyme leaves

1/4 tsp garlic powder

Preheat the oven to 400°F.

Slice the acorn squash in half so that 1 squash makes 2 servings.
Scoop out and discard the seeds. Rub the inside of each squash half
with 1 1/2 tsp of the ghee and sprinkle with salt.

Heat a large skillet over medium heat. Lightly brown the pork in the
skillet, breaking it up with a spatula. (The pork does not need to be
completely cooked through, because it will finish in the oven.)

Using a slotted spoon, remove the pork from the skillet and set
aside. If the pork did not render enough fat to sauté the vegetables,
add the remaining 1 1/2 tsp of ghee to the skillet. Add the carrots,
mushrooms, and onion to the skillet and season with salt and pepper.
Sauté over medium heat until the vegetables start to soften, about
3–5 minutes. Add the pork back to the skillet. Sprinkle on the thyme
and garlic powder and stir to combine.

Fill the squash halves with equal amounts of the filling and place on
a rimmed baking sheet or casserole dish. Bake on the middle rack of
the oven for 30 minutes. Tent the squash with foil to prevent it from
burning, and bake for an additional 15 minutes, or until it is fork-
tender.

sweet potato fries
with homemade ketchup

Serves: 6   Prep time: **30 minutes**   Cook time: **30 minutes, plus 1 1/2–2 hours if making ketchup**

· Dairy-free   · Nut-free   · Egg-free

KETCHUP

(Makes 1 1/2 cups)

2 lbs Roma tomatoes

1/2 yellow onion, chopped

1 cup filtered water

1 tsp ginger powder

2 cloves garlic, minced

3 Tbsp apple cider vinegar

2 1/2 Tbsp fresh lemon juice

1 Tbsp coconut sugar

2 1/2 tsp sea salt

1/2 tsp ground black pepper

1 tsp paprika

FRIES

1 cup duck fat, Rendered Lard (pg 294), or tallow

3 large sweet potatoes, peeled and cut into fry-sized sticks

Sea salt

Make the ketchup: Score each tomato with an X on the top and bottom. Bring a large pot of water to a boil. Boil the tomatoes for 4–5 minutes, until the skins start to buckle. Remove the tomatoes from the boiling water and place in a bowl filled with ice water to stop the cooking process.

Once the tomatoes have cooled, peel away the skins. Cut the tomatoes in half and scrape out the seeds and juices. It's okay if you don't get it all, but remove as much as you can.

In a large saucepan, combine the tomatoes, onion, water, ginger, garlic, vinegar, lemon juice, coconut sugar, salt, pepper, and paprika and simmer for 30 minutes. Smash the tomatoes against the side and bottom of the pan using a large serving fork, then blend using an immersion blender (or standard blender). Return the blended tomatoes to the pot and continue to simmer for 1–2 hours, until the ketchup reaches the desired consistency. Allow to cool to room temperature before serving or bottling. Store the ketchup in a mason jar with a tight-fitting lid in the refrigerator for up to 3 weeks.

To make the fries, heat the duck fat over medium heat, using a candy thermometer to monitor the temperature. Once it reaches 350°F, carefully drop in some sweet potato sticks and fry them until the edges just start to get golden. Remove from the fat and place on a wire rack set over a rimmed baking sheet to drain. Cycle through all of the sweet potatoes, allowing the temperature of the fat to come back up to 350°F between batches. Then return the first batch to the fat and fry again for 1–2 minutes, until golden brown. The second fry will brown them very quickly, so don't blink! Season with salt and serve with the ketchup.

Cook's Note:

Sweet potato fries typically do not get crispy like fries made from white potatoes because they lack the high starch content of white potatoes. However, the double frying technique helps to overcome this disadvantage.

vegetable lo mein

Serves: **6**   Prep time: **15 minutes**   Cook time: **30 minutes**

· Dairy-free   · Nut-free   · Egg-free

2 medium sweet potatoes, peeled and spiral-sliced

4 cloves garlic, minced

1 tsp grated fresh ginger

1/2 onion, sliced

1 Tbsp ghee, store-bought or homemade (pg 286)

1/2 cup Chicken Stock (pg 278)

1/2 tsp red pepper flakes

1/4 cup coconut aminos

2 carrots, peeled and julienned

8 button mushrooms, sliced

3 leaves napa cabbage, julienned

1 (8-oz) can sliced bamboo shoots

1 tsp sea salt

8 grinds black pepper

1 tsp toasted sesame oil

Place the sweet potatoes in a large heatproof mixing bowl. In a large soup pot, bring enough water to cover the sweet potato noodles to a boil. Once the water comes to a full boil, remove from the heat and pour over the noodles. Be sure that all of the noodles are submerged and cover with the lid to the soup pot. Allow the noodles to sit in the hot liquid for 20 minutes, or until they are tender, then drain well.

Meanwhile, over medium-low heat, cook the garlic, ginger, and onion in the ghee. Once the onion begins to soften, approximately 6 minutes, add the stock, red pepper flakes, coconut aminos, carrots, mushrooms, cabbage, bamboo shoots, salt, and pepper. Cover and cook for approximately 10 minutes, stirring occasionally, until all of the veggies are al dente. Add the toasted sesame oil and toss over the heat for 1 more minute.

Toss the sautéed vegetables with the drained sweet potato noodles and serve.

Cook's Note:

To make this recipe nightshade-free, omit the red pepper flakes.

sauces & dressings

caramelized maple balsamic

Yield: **just under 1 cup**   Time needed: **15 minutes**

· Dairy-free   · Nut-free   · Egg-free   · Nightshade-free

 66 This versatile sauce can be used on a variety of different salads. It's also delicious over Maple Vanilla Bean Ice Cream (pg 380). Be sure to watch the temperature closely while making this sauce, as it can thicken quickly after a certain point. For citrus lovers, add extra lemon juice. 99

1/2 cup granulated maple sugar

1/4 cup filtered water

2 Tbsp balsamic vinegar

2 tsp fresh lemon juice

Combine the maple sugar and water in a saucepan over medium-low heat. Stir continuously until the water evaporates to create a thin honeylike consistency; this is caramelizing the maple sugar.

Add the balsamic vinegar and lemon juice to the saucepan. Let the sauce reduce for 5 more minutes, then set aside to cool.

cilantro ginger dressing

Yield: **just under 1 cup**   Time needed: **10 minutes**

· Dairy-free   · Nut-free   · Egg-free   · Nightshade-free

66A soy and ginger dressing really completes an Asian-inspired salad. This dressing will give you all the flavor of a soy-based dressing without the soy. Enjoy it over our Asian Chicken Salad (pg 110) or simply over a bed of mixed greens as a side dish. 99

1/2 cup coconut aminos

1 clove garlic, minced

1 Tbsp grated fresh ginger

Juice of 1/2 lemon (1 1/2 Tbsp)

1/4 tsp sea salt

5 grinds black pepper

1 Tbsp toasted sesame oil

2 Tbsp extra-virgin olive oil

2 Tbsp minced fresh cilantro leaves

In a small mixing bowl, whisk together the coconut aminos, garlic, ginger, lemon juice, salt, and pepper.

Slowly add the sesame oil and olive oil, whisking continuously, then add the cilantro and whisk again.

citrus vinaigrette

Yield: **just under 1 cup**   Time needed: **10 minutes**

· Dairy-free   · Nut-free   · Egg-free

Juice of 1 orange

Juice of 1 lemon (3 Tbsp)

2 Tbsp fig-flavored balsamic vinegar (see Notes)

1/4 tsp sea salt

5 grinds black pepper

1/4 tsp red pepper flakes

1 tsp grated orange zest

1/4 cup extra-virgin olive oil

Serve with Mango and Avocado Salad (pg 208)

Pour the citrus juices into a small mixing bowl. Add the balsamic vinegar, salt, pepper, and red pepper flakes and whisk to combine.

Add the orange zest and whisk again to combine. Slowly add the olive oil to the mixture, whisking continuously.

Keep refrigerated until ready to serve. If the oil separates from the citrus juices, shake or whisk the dressing just before using.

Cook's Notes:

Fig-flavored balsamic vinegar can be hard to come by, although we always seem to find it at our local Whole Foods Market. If you can't find it near you, you can use a raspberry balsamic or regular balsamic vinegar in its place.

To make this recipe nightshade-free, omit the red pepper flakes.

dumpling sauce

Yield: **just over 1/2 cup**   Prep time: **5 minutes**   Cook time: **10 minutes**

· Dairy-free   · Nut-free   · Egg-free

❝ When my sister told me she wanted to make steamed dumplings for this book, I looked at her and said, 'Good luck with that!' She was committed to that recipe, and she mastered it. We loved steamed dumplings as children; they were sure to be included in every order of Chinese food dinners with the family. It is so much fun to be able to enjoy that dish with her again, especially with the sauce! ❞

❝ This sauce was my breakthrough moment in a love-hate relationship with coconut aminos. My career in cooking has involved a lot of soy sauce, so my palate knows that flavor extremely well. I've had many people try to tell me that coconut aminos is the best option for a soy/gluten-free replacement, but I really had to get used to the new flavor profile. When creating this sauce, I learned that the flavor of coconut aminos richens once it is placed over heat, and the addition of balsamic vinegar turned this recipe into a perfect reproduction of my favorite type of dumpling dipping sauce. ❞

1/2 tsp red pepper flakes

1/2 cup coconut aminos

1 tsp balsamic vinegar

1/2 tsp coconut sugar

1/4 tsp fish sauce

Pinch of sea salt

Serve with Pork Dumplings (pg 96)

Grind the red pepper flakes into a powder using a mortar and pestle or food processor. (You can also use a sturdy bowl and the back of a spoon.) The flakes do not need to become a complete powder; you can break them down as far as you like.

In a small saucepan over medium-low heat, whisk together all of the ingredients. Gradually bring up the heat until the sauce begins to scald (steam rises) and the coconut sugar dissolves. Remove from the heat and set aside until ready to serve.

garlic-chive aioli

Yield: **1/4 cup**   Time needed: **10 minutes**

· Dairy-free   · Nightshade-free

❝ The mayonnaise recipe in our first book, *Make it Paleo,* uses macadamia nut oil. It is a delicious and creamy mayonnaise, and the use of macadamia nut oil is perfect because of the mild flavor of that particular oil. I also love using macadamia nut oil as the base for an aioli dipping sauce, because the flavors are fantastic! Try serving this aioli with Salmon Cakes (pg 164). ❞

MACADAMIA NUT MAYONNAISE

(Makes a heaping 1 cup)

1 large egg

2 tsp fresh lemon juice

1/4 tsp sea salt

1/4 tsp ground black pepper

1/4 tsp dry mustard

1 cup extra-virgin macadamia nut oil

GARLIC-CHIVE AIOLI

1/4 cup Macadamia Nut Mayonnaise (above)

Grated zest of 1/2 small lemon

1/4 tsp garlic powder

1 tsp chopped fresh chives

To make the mayonnaise, crack the egg into a 32-oz wide-mouth mason jar. Add the lemon juice, salt, pepper, and dry mustard and blend using an immersion blender.

Once the egg is frothy and fully blended with the seasonings, slowly add the macadamia nut oil with the immersion blender on high. Once all of the oil has been added, you will have a thick, creamy mayonnaise.

Scoop 1/4 cup of the mayo into a small mixing bowl. Add the lemon zest, garlic powder, and chives and gently stir the seasonings into the mayo. Check for seasoning and add additional salt and pepper, if desired.

Cook's Notes:

Some people find that there is no need to drizzle in the oil when using an immersion blender. However, in my experience, sometimes an emulsion will not work, even with an immersion blender, if the oil is added too quickly. You want to be sure that your mayo will turn out well, and you don't want to risk having to dump a cup of expensive oil down the drain, so I recommend adding the oil a little at a time.

To make these recipes nut-free, you can use olive oil in place of the macadamia nut oil.

homemade mayonnaise

Yield: **1 1/4 cups**   Time needed: **10 minutes**

· Dairy-free   · Nut-free   · Nightshade-free

 66 The secret to making perfect mayonnaise from scratch is all in the technique. We've tried making mayo from scratch many different ways, but this is hands down the easiest. To make it, all you need is a large, wide-mouth mason jar and an immersion blender. As a bonus, once the mayo is made, you can store it in the same mason jar! 99

1 large egg (see Note)

1 Tbsp fresh lemon juice

1/4 tsp German mustard

1/3 cup extra-virgin olive oil

1/3 cup cold-pressed sesame oil (untoasted)

1/3 cup coconut oil, melted

1/4 tsp sea salt

1/4 tsp ground black pepper

In a large, wide-mouth mason jar, place the egg, lemon juice, and mustard. Tip the jar to the side and use an immersion blender to process the ingredients until mixed, about 5 seconds.

In a liquid measuring cup, stir together the olive oil, sesame oil, and melted coconut oil.

With the immersion blender running in the jar, very slowly drizzle in the mixed oils. The mixture should thicken as you process it.

Once all of the oil has been added, mix in the salt and pepper. Keep the mayonnaise in the refrigerator; it should be good for up to 5 days.

Cook's Note:

If you are concerned about the use of raw egg in this recipe, you can opt for a pasteurized egg from your local grocery store. It's always important to trust your ingredients, especially if you are going to consume them undercooked or, in this case, raw.

lemon-caper aioli

Yield: **1 cup**   Time needed: **10 minutes**

· Dairy-free   · Nut-free   · Nightshade-free

1 heaping Tbsp capers

2 cloves garlic, minced

2 tsp fresh lemon juice

1 large egg

3/4 cup extra-virgin olive oil

Place the capers, garlic, lemon juice, and egg in a wide-mouth mason jar and blend together using an immersion blender. With the immersion blender running on low speed, very slowly pour in the olive oil in a steady stream to keep the emulsion from breaking. Once all the oil is incorporated, continue to blend for 1–2 minutes to thicken.

lemon vinaigrette

Yield: **1/4 cup**   Time needed: **10 minutes**

· Dairy-free   · Nut-free   · Egg-free   · Nightshade-free

 66 This light and refreshing vinaigrette is my go-to dressing for salads. It's so simple to whip up, and it adds just the right amount of flavor to a salad. It also makes a fantastic marinade for chicken or fish. 99

Juice of 3 small lemons
(1/4 cup plus 2 Tbsp)

1/2 cup extra-virgin olive oil

1/4 tsp sea salt

5 grinds black pepper

Pinch of granulated garlic

1 tsp minced fresh parsley

Pour the lemon juice into a small mixing bowl. Whisk in the olive oil. Season with the salt, pepper, and garlic and whisk to combine.

Add the parsley and whisk again. Pour into a glass jar and refrigerate until ready to use. Shake well before serving.

oyster sauce

Yield: **about 1 cup**   Prep time: **20 minutes**   Cook time: **20 minutes**

· Dairy-free   · Nut-free   · Egg-free   · Nightshade-free

66Adding oyster sauce to Chinese and Thai dishes is a great way to enhance savory flavors. Versions sold in stores are often artificially thickened and have added ingredients like MSG and soy sauce. Since Paleo folks steer clear of those ingredients, we wanted to provide a recipe for making the real thing. You'll be rewarded with a great-tasting sauce that deepens the flavors of your stir-fries and noodle dishes. 99

15 oysters, plus their liquid

1 1/2 tsp filtered water

1 tsp sea salt

2 Tbsp coconut aminos for each 1/2 cup of liquid that remains after the oyster meat has been strained off

Special equipment:

Oyster knife (see Note)

Shuck the oysters by placing the flat side up and carefully inserting an oyster knife into the hinge or "joint" of the oyster. We suggest wearing protective gloves and/or using a towel to hold the oyster securely. Breaking through the hinge can require a little jiggling of the oyster knife. Once open, use the oyster knife to separate the muscle and scrape the meat out of the shell. Reserve the liquid along with the meat.

Mince the oyster meat. Place the meat and reserved liquid in a small saucepan and add the water. Bring to a boil, then reduce the heat and simmer for 10 minutes. Add the salt and allow the mixture to cool. Strain the liquid into another saucepan and discard the meat. Add the coconut aminos to the strained liquid and simmer over medium-low heat for 8 minutes to combine all of the ingredients and enhance the flavor of the sauce.

Cook's Note:

For your safety, make sure that you are using the correct tool; oyster, or shucking, knives can be found in most stores that sell cooking utensils.

"peanut" sauce

Yield: **3/4 cup**   Prep time: **5 minutes**   Cook time: **10 minutes**

· Dairy-free   · Nut-free   · Egg-free

 66 Peanut sauce was one of my favorite dipping sauces as a kid. I especially loved the sweet and spicy flavor of this sauce over chicken. Conventional peanut sauce typically contains corn syrup and soy, so we are delighted to be able to enjoy a healthier version that tastes just like the real thing. Serve it with Summer Spring Rolls (pg 142). 99

1/4 cup sunflower seed butter

1/4 cup filtered water

3 Tbsp coconut aminos

2 Tbsp toasted sesame oil

3 drops fish sauce

1/2 tsp red pepper flakes

1/2 tsp coconut sugar

1/4 tsp garlic powder

1/4 tsp onion powder

In a small saucepan over low heat, combine the sunflower seed butter, water, and coconut aminos. Whisk continuously until smooth.

Add the remaining ingredients and whisk again until combined.

Turn up the heat to medium-low and heat the sauce until it is scalding (steam rising), but not bubbling. Remove from the heat and allow to cool, then refrigerate until ready to use. Allow the sauce to come to room temperature before serving.

pico de gallo

Yield: **1 1/2 cups**   Time needed: **15 minutes**

· Dairy-free   · Nut-free   · Egg-free

❝ If you read all of my recipe introductions in this book, you'll notice a running theme: I'm a sucker for recipes that take some work. I don't know why that is, but I find it oddly soothing to chop a whole bunch of different ingredients. This recipe has that in spades. We use pico to top sunny-side-up eggs, or serve it alongside Carne Asada (pg 72). The bright, fresh flavors pair well with many dishes, so mix some up! ❞

2 ripe Roma tomatoes

1/4 cup minced red onion

1/2 jalapeño, seeded and minced

Juice of 1 lime (2 Tbsp)

3 Tbsp minced fresh cilantro leaves

1/4 tsp sea salt

1/4 tsp ground black pepper

Slice the tomatoes in half and scoop out the seeds with a spoon. Dice the tomato flesh and place it in a medium-sized mixing bowl. Add the onion and jalapeño and pour in the lime juice. Stir in the cilantro, salt, and pepper.

pizza sauce

Yield: **about 1 cup (enough for 2 pizzas)**   Prep time: **10 minutes**   Cook time: **up to 1 hour**

· Dairy-free   · Nut-free   · Egg-free

 66 One of my favorite things to do in the kitchen is bring together a great sauce. Where Hayley and I differ in our cooking styles is that I love to slow down and enjoy the process, while she prefers to work more efficiently. It's just a difference in preference, I suppose. There's no fancy process or secret trick to this recipe, except that you get to stand by the stove and stir it occasionally. I love to taste the developing flavors while the sauce simmers, and I encourage you to do the same; just be careful not to burn yourself! 99

3/4 cup strained tomatoes (see Notes)

3 Tbsp tomato paste

2 tsp dried oregano (see Notes)

3/4 tsp sea salt

1/2 tsp dried marjoram

1/2 tsp garlic powder

1/2 tsp onion powder

1/4 tsp ground black pepper

Place the strained tomatoes in a medium-sized saucepan over medium heat. Whisk in the tomato paste. Stir in the spices and salt. Cook, stirring occasionally, until the sauce begins to bubble, then reduce the heat to low and simmer for up to 1 hour to allow the sauce to reduce slightly.

If not using the sauce immediately, store it in a nonreactive container (such as glass) in the refrigerator for up to 1 week, or ideally freeze it until the day of use. We like to make a batch, split it in half, and save half for later. With a little thawing around the edges of the container, you can pop your Pizza Sauce "ice cube" directly into a small saucepan to warm it.

Cook's Notes:

If possible, select a brand of strained tomatoes with no salt added.

Dried oregano is what gives pizza sauce its signature flavor. Make sure that your dried oregano is relatively new, not something that's been hiding in your cupboard since the late 1990s!

red sauce with a kick

Yield: **2–3 cups**   Prep time: **10 minutes**   Cook time: **20–30 minutes**

· Dairy-free   · Nut-free   · Egg-free

1 Tbsp duck fat

1 cup chopped onion

4 cloves garlic, minced

1 (24-oz) jar strained tomatoes

2 1/2 Tbsp balsamic vinegar

1 tsp dried oregano

1 tsp dried thyme

1 tsp black truffle salt (see Notes)

1/2 tsp ground white pepper

1/8 to 1/4 tsp cayenne pepper (based on heat tolerance)

1 bay leaf

Melt the duck fat in a medium saucepan over medium heat. Add the onion and garlic and sauté, stirring continuously, until the onion starts to turn translucent and begins to caramelize, about 8 minutes.

Add the remaining ingredients, reduce the heat to medium-low, and cook, stirring occasionally, for 20–30 minutes. Your personal preference will factor in when you decide that the sauce is done. For a thicker sauce, simmer until the desired consistency is reached.

Serve warm over grain-free pasta or zucchini noodles. The sauce will keep for up to 1 week in the refrigerator. If storing long-term, allow it to cool before freezing.

Cook's Notes:

This recipe works great with noodles of all sorts (zucchini noodles, Cappello's almond flour pastas, sweet potato noodles, etc.). This sauce is also used in our Baked Eggs with Spaghetti Squash (pg 112), so if you have about a cup left over, save it to make that dish!

Black truffle salt is a special salt blended with tiny bits of black truffles. It is often sold in grocery stores near high-quality cheeses or olives, or with other specialty salts. It packs a strong, earthy truffle flavor that is also a bit pungent. The allure of using truffle salt is to imbue a recipe with the flavor of truffles at a fraction of their cost.

roasted zucchini aioli

Yield: **3/4 cup**   Prep time: **10 minutes**   Cook time: **30 minutes**

· Dairy-free   · Nut-free   · Nightshade-free

1 medium zucchini, seeded and diced

1 Tbsp ghee, store-bought or homemade (pg 286), melted

Sea salt

3 sprigs fresh rosemary

1 clove garlic, smashed with the side of a knife and minced

1 large egg

1 Tbsp fresh lemon juice

5 grinds black pepper

1/2 cup extra-virgin olive oil

Serve with Zucchini Fritters (pg 338)

Preheat the oven to 375°F.

Toss the zucchini with the melted ghee and a pinch of salt and place on a rimmed baking sheet. Top with the rosemary sprigs and roast for 30 minutes.

Remove the zucchini from the oven and discard the rosemary. Place the zucchini in a food processor and process until somewhat smooth.

Place the garlic, egg, lemon juice, pepper, and 1/2 tsp of salt in a wide-mouth mason jar. Using an immersion blender, blend until frothy. With the immersion blender on high, slowly drizzle the olive oil in a steady stream into the mason jar. Once all of the olive oil is blended in and the aioli has emulsified, pour the aioli into a small mixing bowl and fold in the zucchini.

The aioli will keep for up to 5 days in the refrigerator.

smoky barbecue sauce

Yield: **1 1/2 cups**   Prep time: **15 minutes**   Cook time: **1 1/2–2 hours**

· Dairy-free   · Nut-free   · Egg-free

❝A good, clean barbecue sauce is hard to find. Most versions sold in grocery stores contain rogue ingredients like thickeners or high-fructose corn syrup. It's true that barbecue sauce needs something to sweeten it up, but c'mon…leave out the junk! This recipe is easy to pull together and has a great balance of sweetness with a hint of spice and smoke. The chipotle powder, which is made from smoked chiles, gives this sauce a kick. You'll love it! ❞

1 cup Chicken Stock or Beef Stock (pg 278)

1 cup tomato paste

1/4 cup plus 1 Tbsp pure maple syrup

1 Tbsp pure molasses

2 tsp garlic powder

2 tsp chipotle powder, or to taste

1 Tbsp finely grated shallot

Juice of 1/2 lime (1 Tbsp)

1 tsp sea salt

In a medium saucepan, whisk together the stock, tomato paste, maple syrup, and molasses. Set on a small burner over low heat. Stir in the garlic powder and chipotle powder. It's okay to taste the sauce as you go (and encouraged, actually), so go slowly and add the amount of chipotle powder you like.

Add the shallot, lime juice, and salt and simmer gently over low heat until the sauce has reduced by one-quarter, 1 1/2 to 2 hours. Whisk every 10 minutes or so to prevent the sauce at the bottom of the pan from burning.

This sauce will keep in the refrigerator for up to 1 week.

tangy mango sauce

Yield: **about 1 cup**   Prep time: **10 minutes**   Cook time: **20 minutes**

· Dairy-free   · Nut-free   · Egg-free

❝ This sauce is the perfect complement to our Thai Fried Chicken (pg 144). The sweet mango flavor paired with tangy vinegar and pungent garlic creates a sweet and savory accompaniment that goes great over roasted chicken as well. ❞

1 cup white vinegar

2 tsp red pepper flakes

4 cloves garlic, minced

1 1/2 tsp fish sauce

1/4 cup coconut aminos

1 mango, peeled and diced

1 Tbsp coconut sugar

In a small saucepan, combine all of the ingredients. Bring to a boil over medium heat, stirring often.

Reduce the heat to medium-low and simmer for 20 minutes, until the sauce has reduced and thickened slightly. Let the sauce cool slightly, then pulse it in a blender.

Refrigerate until ready to use. This sauce will keep in the refrigerator for up to 2 weeks.

tzatziki

Serves: **4–6**   Time needed: **20 minutes**

· Nut-free   · Egg-free   · Nightshade-free

 ❝"When Bill and I visited Greece, I was so excited to try real, traditional tzatziki, a light, refreshing yogurt sauce. It's most commonly served over gyros, but to me, it's fantastic on absolutely everything. ❞

3/4 cup (6 oz) grass-fed Greek yogurt (see Notes)

Juice of 1/2 lemon (1 1/2 Tbsp)

1/3 cup peeled, seeded, and diced cucumber

1/2 tsp sea salt

3 grinds black pepper

1 clove garlic, pressed

1/4 cup minced fresh dill

Scoop the yogurt into a small mixing bowl. Pour the lemon juice over the yogurt and whisk to combine. Add the cucumber, salt, pepper, and garlic and whisk again.

Add the dill and whisk once more. Use immediately or keep refrigerated until ready to use.

Cook's Notes:

It's best to use this sauce within a day of making it. The water from the cucumbers can affect the texture after a day or so.

If you can't find grass-fed Greek yogurt, you can make your own by lining a mesh strainer with cheesecloth and then pouring regular grass-fed yogurt into the strainer. The liquid from the yogurt will drip through the cheesecloth into a bowl, and you will be left with thick, creamy yogurt.

For a nondairy version, you can use an unsweetened version of the Coconut Milk Yogurt on pg 276; just follow the first four steps and be sure to omit the cherries and vanilla.

walnut pesto

Yield: **about 1 cup**   Time needed: **10 minutes**

· Dairy-free   · Egg-free   · Nightshade-free

1/3 cup raw walnuts

1 clove garlic, smashed with the side of a knife

2 packed cups fresh basil leaves

1/2 cup extra-virgin olive oil

Juice of 1/2 lemon (1 1/2 Tbsp)

1/2 tsp sea salt

10 grinds black pepper

In a food processor, pulse the walnuts and garlic until evenly chopped. Add the basil and continue to pulse.

With the processor running, add the olive oil, lemon juice, salt, and pepper and blend until smooth.

Use immediately, refrigerate for up to 4–5 days, or freeze for longer-term storage.

nut-free pesto

Yield: **1 cup**   Time needed: **10 minutes**

· Dairy-free   · Nut-free   · Egg-free   · Nightshade-free

1/3 cup raw sunflower seeds

1 clove garlic, smashed with the side of a knife

2 packed cups fresh basil leaves

1/2 cup extra-virgin olive oil

Juice of 1/2 lemon (1 1/2 Tbsp)

1/2 tsp sea salt

10 grinds black pepper

In a food processor, pulse the sunflower seeds and garlic until evenly chopped. Add the basil and continue to pulse.

With the processor running, add the olive oil, lemon juice, salt, and pepper and blend until smooth.

Use immediately, refrigerate for up to 4–5 days, or freeze for longer-term storage.

basics & projects

1. salty rib rub

2 Tbsp Adobo Seasoning
(pg 272)

1 Tbsp sea salt

1 tsp ground turmeric

1 tsp Tandoori Seasoning
(pg 273)

1 tsp onion powder

1 tsp paprika

1 tsp dried oregano

1/2 tsp garlic powder

2. sweet pork rub

2 Tbsp coconut sugar

1 1/2 tsp paprika

1 tsp onion powder

1 tsp garlic powder

1 tsp pink Himalayan salt

1/2 tsp ground cumin

1/2 tsp dried oregano

1/4 tsp ground white pepper

1/4 tsp chipotle powder

3. thai rub

1 tsp ground lemongrass

1/2 tsp Thai basil

1/2 tsp onion powder

1/2 tsp garlic powder

1/2 tsp ground cumin

1/2 tsp cayenne pepper

1/2 tsp dried lemon peel

1/2 tsp ground black pepper

1/2 tsp pink Himalayan salt

1/4 tsp coconut sugar

1/4 tsp ginger powder

4. adobo seasoning

1 Tbsp pink Himalayan salt

1 Tbsp granulated garlic

2 tsp dried oregano

1 tsp ground black pepper

1 tsp onion powder

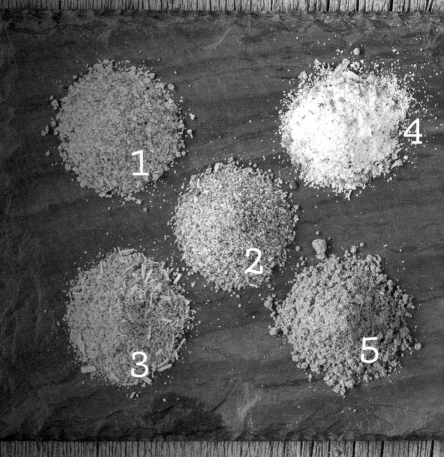

5. moroccan rib rub

1 Tbsp Ras el Hanout (pg 273)

1/2 tsp ground turmeric

1/2 tsp pink Himalayan salt

1/2 tsp ground black pepper

1/4 tsp pulverized bay leaf

6. barbacoa spice mix

1 Tbsp kosher salt
2 tsp paprika
1 tsp ground cumin
1 tsp dried oregano
1/4 tsp chipotle powder

8. tandoori seasoning

1 tsp ground ginger
1 tsp ground cumin
1 tsp sea salt
1 tsp cayenne pepper
1 tsp ground coriander
1 tsp paprika
1 tsp ground turmeric

9. ras el hanout

2 tsp ginger powder
2 tsp ground mace
2 tsp ground cardamom
1 tsp ground turmeric
1 tsp ground nutmeg
1 tsp ground coriander
1 tsp ground allspice
1 tsp ground cinnamon
1/2 tsp ground black pepper
1/2 tsp ground white pepper
1/2 tsp cayenne pepper
1/2 tsp ground anise

10. poultry blend

1 tsp garlic powder
1 tsp onion powder
1 tsp dried oregano
1/2 tsp pink Himalayan salt
1/2 tsp ground turmeric
1/2 tsp paprika
1/4 tsp chili powder
1/4 tsp ground black pepper

7. greek gyro seasoning

1 Tbsp dried oregano
1 tsp dried marjoram
1 tsp dried thyme
1/2 tsp ground cumin
1/2 tsp sea salt
1/2 tsp ground black pepper

baking powder

Yield: **1/2 cup**   Time needed: **5 minutes**

- Dairy-free   - Nut-free   - Egg-free   - Nightshade-free

"Baking powder is a fundamental ingredient for baking. It's a leavening agent, which means that it helps baked goods like cakes, cookies, and cupcakes rise. Store-bought baking powder commonly contains an anticlumping agent, usually cornstarch, although we've found a brand that uses potato starch instead. I wanted to make a homemade version for this book so that folks who cannot consume potato starch can still enjoy baking with baking powder. Homemade baking powder seems to be more effective at making baked goods rise, too. Have fun trying out this recipe and watching that magic happen!"

1/4 cup cream of tartar

2 Tbsp baking soda

2 Tbsp tapioca starch or arrowroot starch

Pour the ingredients into a 6- to 8-oz glass jar.

Stir with a spoon to blend the ingredients evenly, then seal the jar tightly with the lid and shake a bit, just to be sure that everything is really well combined.

Cook's Note:

Use this homemade baking powder in any recipe that calls for baking powder. Store baking powder in a sealed glass container in a cool, dry place. It is will keep for up to 18 months.

cherry vanilla coconut milk yogurt

Serves: **4**   Prep time: **1 hour**   Ferment time: **12–15 hours**   Chill time: **6 1/2–7 hours**

· Dairy-free   · Nut-free   · Egg-free   · Nightshade-free

YOGURT

(Makes 5 cups)

2 1/2 tsp grass-fed beef gelatin

1/4 cup cold filtered water

3 (13 1/2-oz) cans full-fat coconut milk, chilled

2 Tbsp pure maple syrup

1 package dairy-free yogurt starter

CHERRY VANILLA BLEND

1 cup frozen, pitted cherries, defrosted

2 tsp pure vanilla extract

Special equipment:

Yogurt maker

Clean and sterilize the glass jars that come with your yogurt maker. (Ours comes with seven 6-oz jars.)

Pour the gelatin into a small mixing bowl and cover with the cold water to "bloom" the gelatin. This will help the gelatin dissolve evenly into the coconut milk.

Remove the cans of coconut milk from the fridge and open them from the bottom. The cream will have risen to the top, and all of the water will be on the bottom. Discard the water and scoop the thick cream into a medium-sized saucepan. Attach a candy thermometer to the side of the pan and place the pan over medium heat. Heat the coconut milk to 180°F, then remove it from the heat. Whisk in the gelatin and maple syrup and continue whisking until the gelatin is completely dissolved into the hot coconut milk.

Allow the coconut milk to cool to 115°F. Once cooled to the proper temperature, pour it into a 1-quart glass liquid measuring cup or other glass container with a spout to assist in pouring. Whisk the yogurt starter into the coconut milk and pour into the sterilized glass jars. Place in a yogurt maker and ferment according to the manufacturer's instructions for 12–15 hours.

After 12 hours, the yogurt should smell sour and appear to have solidified slightly. The cream may separate from any additional water that remained in the coconut milk during the fermentation process. This is okay. Tightly seal the jars and place in the fridge for 6 hours to allow the gelatin to set up. After 6 hours, pour the yogurt into a high-speed blender and pulse until it is a traditional creamy consistency. Place the yogurt back in the fridge for another 30–60 minutes to set once more.

Meanwhile, in a high-speed blender or food processor, pulse the cherries and vanilla extract. Top the cherry vanilla blend with 2 cups of the plain yogurt, stir to combine and serve. There will be plain yogurt left over to use as you wish.

Cook's Notes:

If you can't tolerate any dairy, this coconut milk-based yogurt is a great option to use in place of yogurt in any sweet or savory recipe.

This recipe can be used to make a nondairy version of our Tzatziki (pg 266); just omit the cherry and vanilla mixture, but not the maple syrup! That sugar is what feeds the yogurt starter culture and makes the yogurt sour.

chicken stock and beef stock

Yield: **2 quarts each**   Prep time: **15 minutes**   Cook time: **15 hours**

· Dairy-free   · Nut-free   · Egg-free   · Nightshade-free

CHICKEN STOCK

3 pounds chicken backs

1 pound chicken thigh bones (reserved from cooking chicken thighs)

1 Tbsp apple cider vinegar

1 Vidalia onion, peeled and quartered

1 bunch celery with leaves, roughly chopped

4 medium carrots, peeled and chopped

4 cloves garlic

1 Tbsp black peppercorns

2 tsp pink Himalayan salt

BEEF STOCK

2 1/2 lbs beef knuckle and marrow bones

1 Tbsp apple cider vinegar

1 Vidalia onion, peeled and quartered

1 bunch celery with leaves, roughly chopped

4 medium carrots, peeled and chopped

1 Tbsp black peppercorns

2 tsp pink Himalayan salt

1 bay leaf

Place the backs (if making chicken stock) and bones in a Dutch oven or stockpot. Pour the vinegar over the bones.

Add the vegetables, garlic (if making chicken stock), peppercorns, salt, and bay leaf (if making beef stock) to the pot. Pour enough filtered water over the bones and vegetables to cover them completely.

Turn on the heat to medium and stir. Bring the stock to a boil, then reduce the heat to a simmer. Simmer the stock, uncovered, for 15 hours. After 5–7 hours, taste it every hour to make sure that none of the veggies are burning, which would give the stock a bitter taste.

Strain the fully cooked stock through a fine-mesh strainer and pour the strained stock into two 1-quart mason jars. Keep in the fridge for up to 1 week if using immediately, or freeze until ready to use.

Discard the layer of fat on top before using the stock in soups or stews.

Cook's Notes:

For even better flavor, you can roast the bones for 30 minutes before starting your stock, which will bring out the flavors of the bones in the stock. This is why we love using bones left over from a roast or roasting chickens—the roasting work is already done!

You can also make this stock in a slow cooker, but we prefer stovetop cooking if you have a gas stove, because it yields more even heat and prevents the vegetables from burning. If using a slow cooker, monitor the stock to make sure that none of the vegetables are burning.

cured bacon

Yield: **15 pounds**   Prep time: **30 minutes, plus 2 hours to smoke**   Cure time: **1 week**   Chill time: **12 hours**

· Dairy-free   · Nut-free   · Egg-free   · Nightshade-free

 ❝This recipe is heavily inspired by Michael Ruhlman's recipe for bacon in his beloved book *Charcuterie*. Curing meat is a craft that used to be passed down from generation to generation but is getting lost and forgotten with the widespread availability of prepackaged foods. I love Ruhlman's simple, no-nonsense approach to all things food, and also his work toward sustaining traditional food knowledge. With my version, I've provided quantities for what most people might consider a triple batch—15 pounds! You can start off with a 5-pound slab, but don't say I didn't warn you that it won't be enough. ❞

3/4 cup coarse sea salt or kosher salt

6 tsp pink curing salt or celery juice powder (see Note)

1/2 cup pure maple syrup

1/4 cup granulated maple sugar

1/2 cup ground black pepper

6 bay leaves, crumbled

15 lbs pork belly, cut into 1-lb pieces

15 cloves garlic, smashed with the side of a knife

Combine the coarse sea salt, pink curing salt, maple syrup, maple sugar, and spices in a medium-sized mixing bowl. Rub the mixture all over the pieces of pork belly and place in zip-top plastic bags along with the garlic, 1 clove for each pound of belly. Refrigerate for 7 days. Flip the bags daily to ensure even contact with the dry rub.

After 7 days, remove the belly from the bags and rinse under cold water. Pat dry with a paper towel.

If you have a smoker, smoke the belly for 2 hours at 200–220°F. Otherwise, cook the belly in a 200°F oven for 90 minutes. With either method, the bacon should reach an internal temperature of 150°F.

Refrigerate for 12 hours or freeze. Slice into strips, cook as you would any other bacon, and serve.

Cook's Note:

Pink curing salt is sodium nitrite, which is not *the same as pink Himalayan salt. Take care to purchase the right product. Pink curing salt helps the bacon retain its bright pink color during cooking. If you omit the pink curing salt or celery juice powder, the bacon will turn brown while cooking and will taste more like seasoned pork. The pink curing salt or celery juice powder is essential to the curing process. It produces nitrates that help fend off the bad bacteria that can manifest during the curing process. Nitrates in food are not to be feared, especially in the minute amounts present in cured meats. Emerging evidence has linked nitrates to certain health benefits. If you are interested, Chris Kresser has a comprehensive post on the subject at ChrisKresser.com. Both pink curing salt and celery juice powder can be ordered online, and specialty food stores may carry them as well.*

cured salmon

Yield: **1 pound**   Prep time: **15 minutes**   Cure time: **24 hours**

· Dairy-free   · Nut-free   · Egg-free   · Nightshade-free

❝When I signed on to this project, one of the first things Hayley requested of me was that I create several fish dishes. I decided that the best place to start would be at the most simple and fish-centric place: cured fish. This recipe is easy to execute, especially if you have a reliable source for fresh fish. This cured salmon is best served thinly sliced and can be enjoyed on its own, with capers, on a salad, or with most breakfast dishes. ❞

CURE MIXTURE

1/4 cup fennel seeds

Grated zest of 3 lemons

1/4 cup plus 1 Tbsp granulated maple sugar

1/4 cup rubbed sage

2 cups kosher salt

1 (1-lb) fresh, wild-caught salmon fillet, cut in half

Place all of the ingredients for the cure mixture in a food processor and process until evenly combined.

Place the salmon in a loaf pan or similar-sized vessel. Bury the salmon in the cure mixture so that it is completely covered. Cover with plastic wrap and place a heavy object (such as a brick or heavy jar) on top. Allow to cure in the refrigerator for 24 hours.

Rinse the salmon under cold water, slice into strips, and serve.

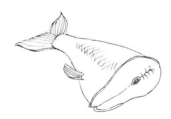

dashi

Yield: **over 2 quarts**   Prep time: **10 minutes**   Cook time: **45 minutes**

· Dairy-free   · Nut-free   · Egg-free   · Nightshade-free

 ❝Dashi is the foundation of many Japanese soups and dishes. It is a versatile fish stock that not only is easy to make, but also provides wonderful flavor. Few ingredients are needed to make dashi. Whole Foods typically carries kombu (dried kelp) and katsuobushi (bonito flakes). I purchase mine at my local Japanese grocer because I can get them in larger quantities. If you love dishes that are packed with flavor, use Ichiban (first batch) dashi in place of a lightly flavored stock, yielding a smokier flavor. ❞

4 (4-by-4-inch) pieces kombu

9 cups filtered water, divided

66 grams katsuobushi (bonito flakes; see Note)

Rinse the kombu under cold water. Place it in a medium-sized pot along with 4 1/2 cups of water and simmer for 30 minutes. Remove from the heat, remove the kombu from the water, and set the kombu aside for Niban dashi.

Add the katsuobushi to the still-hot water and allow it to hydrate; you may need to give it a light push into the water if some is still sitting dry on the top after a few minutes. Once all of the katsuobushi is hydrated, remove it from the water by pouring the liquid through a strainer into a bowl, and reserve it for the Niban dashi. This first batch of liquid is Ichiban dashi and can be used as a strong, smoky fish stock.

In a medium-sized pot, combine the reserved kombu with 4 1/2 cups of fresh filtered water. Bring to a simmer and gently cook for 5 minutes. Remove from the heat, add the reserved katsuobushi, and allow to steep for 5 more minutes. Strain the kombu and katsuobushi from the liquid and discard. The remaining stock is Niban dashi, a light fish stock.

Combine the Ichiban dashi and the Niban dashi to create a tasty, smoky blended dashi that works well as a fish stock in most recipes.

Cook's Note:

Working by weight is the most accurate way to measure katsuobushi, a light and fluffy ingredient.

ghee

Yield: **about 1 cup**   Time needed: **20 minutes**

· Dairy-free   · Nut-free   · Egg-free   · Nightshade-free

"Ghee is simply butter with the milk solids removed, so all you are left with is a cooking fat. It is perfect for people who love butter but cannot tolerate the lactose in dairy. You can use ghee for sautéing, roasting, and baking as well!"

1 cup (2 sticks) unsalted grass-fed butter

Roughly cube the butter and place it in a medium-sized saucepan. Bring to a boil over medium-high heat, stirring continuously. A foamy layer will form on top.

Turn down the heat to medium-low and reduce the frequency of stirring. You will notice the milk solids separating to the bottom of the pan and the liquid becoming clearer and more golden.

After about 8–10 minutes, a second foaming will occur. Once the second foam layer covers the liquid, the ghee is ready for straining. Using a fine-mesh strainer and several layers of cheesecloth, strain the ghee into a small mixing bowl. For ultraclear ghee, pour the strained ghee through new cheesecloth to strain it a second time.

Pour the ghee into a lidded container and refrigerate, if desired.

ginger beer

Yield: **2 liters**   Prep time: **1 1/2 hours**   Ferment time: **1–2 days**

· Dairy-free   · Nut-free   · Egg-free   · Nightshade-free

"Ginger beer is a fun food project. Unlike fermenting kombucha, the fermentation process for ginger beer is just to develop carbonation and takes only 48 hours. The nearly instant feedback makes the process fun. Before you know it, you'll be enjoying your first Moscow Mule (pg 308) with home-brewed ginger beer!"

1 (3-oz) piece of fresh ginger (about the width of your palm)

3/4 cup raw cane sugar (see Note)

Filtered water

Juice of 1 small lemon (2 Tbsp), divided

1/4 tsp champagne yeast (also called dry wine yeast), divided

Special equipment:

Two 1-liter bottles with flip-tops

Cook's Note:

Similar to the process of fermenting home-brewed kombucha, it is important to provide the right "food" to fuel the yeast growth and ferment the ginger beer. Raw cane sugar is a good choice for this type of fermentation.

Peel the skin from the ginger. Process the ginger in a food processor until ground into a pulp.

In a small saucepan over medium heat, combine the ginger pulp, sugar, and 3/4 cup of filtered water. Whisk and bring to a light boil, stirring frequently. After 10 minutes, remove the syrup from the heat and allow to steep and cool for 1 hour.

Press the syrup through a very-fine-mesh strainer with a large spoon, separating it from the ginger pulp. Save the syrup and discard the pulp. You should have approximately 2/3 cup of syrup.

Prepare the flip-top bottles. If using 1-liter bottles, use a funnel to pour equal amounts of the ginger syrup into each bottle. Add to each bottle 1 Tbsp of the lemon juice and 1/8 tsp of the champagne yeast, then fill the bottles with filtered water to within an inch of the top. Cap the bottles and give them a shake to mix. Allow the ginger beer to ferment for 1–2 days in a dark, relatively warm place, like a cabinet adjacent to a refrigerator or dishwasher. Depending on the ambient conditions (heat and light), this process could be slow or quick, so for your first attempt, carefully pop the top after 24 hours to check the carbonation.

Once the ginger beer has developed the amount of carbonation you prefer, transfer the bottles to the refrigerator to stop the fermentation process. The ginger beer will keep in the refrigerator for 1–2 weeks.

pickled burdock root

Serves: **1–2**   Prep time: **15 minutes**   Pickling time: **at least 8 hours**

· Dairy-free   · Nut-free   · Egg-free

"Burdock is a root vegetable that historically has been used for its medicinal qualities in Asian cultures. In its most concentrated form, such as an oil, it is a powerful diuretic and great for removing toxins from the blood. In addition to having medicinal purposes, it also happens to be delicious in its root form. When pickled, the root is great for snacking and makes an incredible addition to any salad. It's also a wonderful component to include on a charcuterie board."

1 burdock root (about 10 inches long)

2 Tbsp coconut aminos, divided

5 tsp toasted sesame oil, divided

1/2 tsp red pepper flakes, divided

2 cloves garlic, sliced, divided

1 cup apple cider vinegar, divided

Peel and julienne the burdock. Place in a medium-sized saucepan with water to cover the burdock. Bring to a boil, let simmer for 3 minutes, then drain the burdock over a bowl, reserving the liquid.

Have on hand 2 pint-sized mason jars. In each jar, combine 1 Tbsp of the coconut aminos, 2 1/2 tsp of the toasted sesame oil, 1/4 tsp of the red pepper flakes, half of the garlic slices, 1/2 cup of the vinegar, and half of the boiled burdock root. Fill the rest of each jar with the reserved liquid from boiling the burdock, cover, and refrigerate overnight, or for at least 8 hours.

powdered sugar

Yield: **1 cup**   Time needed: **10 minutes**

· Dairy-free   · Nut-free   · Egg-free   · Nightshade-free

 66Homemade powdered sugar, also called confectioners' sugar, is pretty simple to make. All you need to do is take your choice of unrefined granulated sugar and pulse it in a food processor until it is a fine powder. You can use homemade powdered sugar in place of store-bought powdered sugar for our Vanilla Buttercream Frosting (pg 394); just know that if you do, the frosting will have a tan color to it. 99

1 cup granulated maple sugar or coconut sugar

1 Tbsp tapioca starch

Place the sugar in a high-speed blender or food processor.

Add the tapioca starch and place the lid on the blender. Cover the top of the blender with a kitchen towel to keep sugar dust from getting into the air.

Blend on high speed until the sugar is finely ground, about 30 seconds. Pour the powdered sugar into a glass container for storage or use immediately.

rendered lard

Yield: **about 2 cups**   Prep time: **5 minutes**   Cook time: **2 hours**

· Dairy-free   · Nut-free   · Egg-free   · Nightshade-free

 66Rendering your own lard is so incredibly simple. All you need is pork fat, a heavy skillet, and some time. The result will blow you away. Freshly rendered lard is so creamy and flavorful, you'll wonder why you ever bought other fats to cook with. 99

2 lbs pork back fat

Coarsely chop the back fat so that it will fit in your food processor, then process it into a fine grind. (If you don't have a food processor, chop the fat into the smallest pieces possible.) There will be pieces of different sizes, which is okay. If you want to make crispy lardons from the fat after it has rendered, take a little extra time and carefully chop the fat by hand into tiny cubes.

Place the finely ground fat in a heavy pot and warm over low heat. The fat will render out in a clear liquid. Every 30–60 minutes, carefully pour the rendered fat through a strainer into a mason jar, and allow the fat to continue to render. After about 2 hours, drain the last of the rendered fat into the mason jar. At this point, you have lard! Lard can be kept refrigerated for months, though you might use it much faster.

To make lardons, sprinkle a little salt onto the fat in the pot and increase the heat to medium. Stir for 5–10 minutes, until GBD (golden brown and delicious). Drain on a paper plate or paper towel laid over a wire rack. You can top your favorite dish with the lardons or save them in the refrigerator for 3–4 days.

tomato jam

Yield: **1 quart**　Prep time: **20 minutes**　Cook time: **1 1/2–2 hours**

· Nut-free　· Egg-free

❝Slightly different from traditional sweet, fruity jams, tomato jam works great on our Grain-Free Sandwich Bread (pg 324) or with sausage at breakfast. It's also great over rice crackers with goat cheese. For those who love a sweeter jam, feel free to double the amount of sugar; this recipe does well with increased sugar.❞

15 Roma tomatoes, halved and seeded

1/2 cup finely diced yellow onion

1 Tbsp unsalted grass-fed butter

1 Tbsp plus 2 tsp balsamic vinegar

2 Tbsp plus 1 tsp granulated maple sugar

1 1/2 tsp sea salt

Juice of 1 lemon (3 Tbsp)

7 grinds black pepper

1/2 tsp ground cinnamon

Pinch of red pepper flakes

Place the tomatoes in a food processor and process into small chunks.

In a saucepan over medium-low heat, caramelize the onion in the butter until light brown, about 20 minutes. Add the tomatoes and the remaining ingredients and simmer for 1 1/2–2 hours, stirring periodically, until the jam has reduced by about half and is thick, like a very thick tomato sauce. It will keep for 2–3 weeks in the refrigerator.

Cook's Note:

To make this recipe dairy-free, use ghee or lard instead of butter.

drinks

basic nut milk

Yield: **1 quart**   Time needed: **10 minutes, plus at least 8 hours to soak the nuts and dates**

· Dairy-free   · Egg-free   · Nightshade-free

12 oz raw almonds, cashews, or hazelnuts

4 Medjool dates, pitted

Pinch of sea salt

8 cups filtered water, divided

1/2 tsp pure vanilla extract (optional)

Place the nuts, dates, and salt in a medium-sized mixing bowl. Cover with 4 cups of filtered water, or enough that the nuts and dates are completely submerged. Allow to soak overnight, or for at least 8 hours.

After the nuts and dates have soaked, drain and rinse them with cold, fresh water. Pour the nuts and dates into a food processor or high-speed blender and cover with 4 cups of filtered water. Blend on high speed until smooth. If you would like a sweeter-tasting nut milk, add the vanilla extract and blend again for about 30 seconds.

Once the nuts and dates are completely blended with the water, strain the pulp from the milk using a nut milk straining bag or a fine-mesh strainer lined with cheesecloth. Squeeze the pulp in the straining bag to make sure that you get all of the milk out of the pulp. For ultrasmooth milk, strain it again (see Note). Store the nut milk in the refrigerator, and use it within 2–3 days.

Cook's Note:

It is optimal to strain the nut milk at least twice, the first time to strain the milk from the bulk of the pulp, then again to be sure that you have removed all remnants of pulp so that your nut milk is very smooth.

chocolate banana milkshake

Serves: **2–4**   Time needed: **10 minutes**

· Dairy-free   · Egg-free   · Nightshade-free

66 This is a perfect creamy milkshake, without the cream and milk! Bring your favorite ice cream shop treat home with this simple and guilt-free recipe. 99

2 bananas, frozen

1/2 cup ice

1/2 avocado, peeled and pitted

2 cups almond milk (pg 300)

1/4 cup pure maple syrup

1/2 tsp pure vanilla extract

1/4 cup cocoa powder

TOPPING (optional)

Whipped Coconut Cream (pg 398)

Sliced banana

1-2 teaspoons crushed semisweet chocolate

Chop the frozen bananas into large chunks and place in a high-speed blender. Add the ice and pulse for 30 seconds. Add the avocado and pulse again to combine.

Pour in the almond milk, maple syrup, and vanilla extract and blend on high speed until you have a thick, creamy shake.

Add the cocoa powder and blend again until the cocoa powder is completely blended into the shake and the shake is smooth and creamy. If desired, top with the whipped Coconut Cream, sliced bananas, and crushed chocolate.

coconut milk cortado

Serves: **1**   Time needed: **15 minutes**

· Dairy-free   · Nut-free   · Egg-free   · Nightshade-free

"A cortado (derived from the Spanish verb *cortar,* which means "to cut") is a drink made with a one-to-one ratio of espresso to milk. I prefer mine with much thicker and more satisfying coconut cream. Pulling the perfect shot of espresso (or even a really good one) takes a lot of practice. A great shot begins with high-quality espresso beans. Try to purchase beans that have been roasted within the last week. A good roaster will put the roasting date in plain sight on the package. I really like beans from roasters like Verve (California) and La Colombe (Pennsylvania), but you should be able to find good coffee roasters locally. "

12-15 grams very finely ground espresso (see Notes)

2-3 oz full-fat coconut milk or coconut cream

3 drops liquid stevia (optional)

Special equipment:

Espresso machine with portafilter

Warm your portafilter with hot water from the espresso machine. This will give your shot heat stability.

Once the portafilter is warm, add the ground espresso, level it off, and tamp it down firmly, giving it a twist at the end to help level the tamp. Pour or scoop 2–3 oz of coconut milk into a mug (see Notes), along with any sweetener you wish (I like a few drops of liquid stevia). Pull the shot into the mug. Ideally, this should take 20–25 seconds. A rich crema on top means that the beans are fresh and the oils have been properly extracted. Allow the drink to rest for 30 seconds, then stir and enjoy!

Cook's Notes:

Grind your beans very finely, almost to a "Turkish" grade. If you do not have a conical burr grinder, which is necessary for grinding espresso, then buy some preground Illy or Lavazza brand espresso.

The "dose" of espresso is typically measured in grams for accuracy, though you'll hardly ever see a professional barista whip out a scale. After measuring it out a few times, you'll know the correct amount by sight.

For the sake of simplicity, my preferred method is to use room-temperature or even chilled coconut milk for this drink. This temperature allows me to drink the espresso quickly, in true Italian fashion. If you like a piping-hot drink or like to sip slowly, you may prefer to heat the coconut milk before pulling the shot.

hot cocoa

Serves: **4**   Prep time: **10 minutes**   Cook time: **20 minutes**

· Dairy-free   · Nut-free   · Egg-free   · Nightshade-free

3 oz allergen-free semisweet chocolate chips

1 (13 1/2-oz) can full-fat coconut milk

1 tsp pure vanilla extract

2 Tbsp cocoa powder, plus more for dusting

1 Tbsp granulated maple sugar

1/4 tsp ground cinnamon

TOPPING (optional)

Whipped Coconut Cream (pg 398)

If you plan to make the Whipped Coconut Cream topping, place a metal bowl in the freezer to chill.

Place the chocolate chips in a medium-sized saucepan over low heat. Once they start to melt, add the coconut milk and turn up the heat to medium-low. Whisk the chocolate and coconut milk together as the milk begins to warm.

Once the chocolate is mostly melted into the milk, add the vanilla extract, cocoa powder, maple sugar, and cinnamon. Continue to whisk until the mixture is a dark chocolate color, all of the cocoa powder and sugar has dissolved, and the cocoa is thick and creamy.

Turn the heat down to low and simmer the cocoa for 10 minutes, stirring every so often.

While the cocoa is simmering, make the Whipped Coconut Cream, if desired. Serve the hot cocoa with a dollop of Whipped Coconut Cream and a dusting of cocoa powder.

moscow mule

Serves: **1**   Time needed: **3 minutes**

· Dairy-free   · Nut-free   · Egg-free   · Nightshade-free

 ❝Having a Moscow Mule says 'summertime' to me. This particular drink was popular during the 1950s and has experienced a resurgence in recent years. Like many others, I love the refreshing combination of ginger beer and lime juice. If you've experimented with our Ginger Beer recipe (pg 288), this is a great way to fully test it out. My favorite vodka brand to use is Three Hunters Vodka, a Paleo-friendly version of the spirit distilled from grapes and blueberries. ❞

1/2 lime

2 oz vodka

4 oz Ginger Beer (pg 288)

Sprig of fresh mint, for garnish (optional)

Lime wedges, for garnish (optional)

HARVEST MULE
VARIATION

1/2 lime

2 oz vodka

2 oz pure apple cider

2 oz Ginger Beer (pg 288)

Fresh grated cinnamon, for garnish (optional)

KENTUCKY MULE
VARIATION

1/2 lime

2 oz bourbon

4 oz Ginger Beer (pg 288)

Squeeze the juice of half a lime into a glass or mug. Add a few ice cubes and the vodka (or vodka and apple cider if making the Harvest Mule variation, or bourbon if making the Kentucky Mule variation). Finish with the ginger beer, stir, and garnish as desired. Serve cold.

Cook's Note:

A Moscow Mule is typically served in a copper mug, as shown, but you can serve this drink in any container. A Collins glass is another good choice.

natural soda syrups

Serves: **6**   Time needed: **10 minutes, plus at least 8 hours to extract the fruit juices**

· Dairy-free   · Nut-free   · Egg-free   · Nightshade-free

MANGO-GINGER SYRUP

1 mango, peeled and chopped

2 tsp grated fresh ginger

1 1/2 Tbsp fresh lemon juice

2 Tbsp raw honey

BLACKBERRY-LAVENDER SYRUP

12 oz blackberries (about 2 cups)

1 Tbsp dried lavender flowers

1 1/2 Tbsp fresh lemon juice

2 Tbsp raw honey

POMEGRANATE-BLUEBERRY SYRUP

Seeds of 1 pomegranate

6 oz blueberries (about 1 scant cup)

1 1/2 Tbsp fresh lemon juice

2 Tbsp raw honey

Soda water

Place all of the ingredients for your desired syrup in a mason jar and shake vigorously to combine. Place in the refrigerator overnight to extract the juices, or for at least 8 hours.

Remove the jar from the refrigerator and shake well. Strain the solids and use as a fruit spread or discard.

To make your drink, combine 1–2 Tbsp of the syrup with soda water over ice. For a sweeter drink, add more honey or stevia.

The syrups can be stored for up to 2 weeks in the refrigerator.

pumpkin spice latte

Serves: **2**   Prep time: **10 minutes**   Cook time: **10–15 minutes**

· Dairy-free   · Egg-free   · Nightshade-free

"Pumpkin spice lattes are all the rage in the fall. Unfortunately, when purchased at a coffee shop, they often contain undesirable ingredients. This recipe is a healthier alternative for those who want to enjoy this classic autumn drink."

2 cups almond milk
(pg 300)

1/4 cup coconut sugar

1/2 tsp pumpkin pie spice

1/2 tsp pure vanilla extract
(see Note)

1 cup hot strong-brewed
coffee or 2 shots of
espresso

Ground cinnamon, for
garnish

Pour the almond milk into a small saucepan. Add the coconut sugar, pumpkin pie spice, and vanilla extract. Turn on the burner to medium-low heat and whisk until the spices and sugar are completely dissolved into the almond milk.

Warm the spiced almond milk until it starts to bubble, whisking every so often. Allow it to lightly bubble for about 10–15 minutes, or as long as you need to brew the coffee or make the espresso.

Divide the coffee equally between two latte mugs (1/2 cup of coffee per mug) and top with the spiced almond milk (1 cup per mug). Sprinkle with ground cinnamon and enjoy!

Cook's Note:

If you added vanilla extract to your almond milk, then you don't need to add it to this recipe. If you are using plain almond milk, then the vanilla extract in this recipe is important for flavor.

raspberry lemonade

Serves: **6**   Time needed: **10 minutes, plus 1–2 hours to thaw the raspberries**

· Dairy-free   · Nut-free   · Egg-free   · Nightshade-free

❝Fresh lemonade is one of my favorite drinks on a hot summer day. The raspberries not only add a wonderful flavor to a classic drink, but also make the color bright, bold, and beautiful. ❞

Juice of 8 lemons (1 1/2 cups)

1 (10-oz) package frozen raspberries

4 cups filtered water

Liquid stevia extract or sweetener of choice

Fresh raspberries, for garnish (optional)

Fresh basil or mint sprigs, for garnish (optional)

Pour the lemon juice into a mixing bowl. Add the raspberries and let stand for 1–2 hours, stirring every so often, until the raspberries have thawed and combined with the lemon juice.

Pass the fruit mixture through a very-fine-mesh strainer, discarding the pulp and seeds.

Add the fruit juice to a large pitcher and mix with the filtered water. Add liquid stevia extract to taste.

Serve over ice, garnished with fresh raspberries and a sprig of basil or mint, if desired.

sangria

Serves: **4–6**   Prep time: **15 minutes**   Cook time: **15 minutes**

· Dairy-free   · Nut-free   · Egg-free   · Nightshade-free

"Most sangrias are far too sweet for my palate, but this recipe is the perfect balance of fresh citrus, crisp wine, and a mellow hint of ginger at the end. The spiced rum and ginger syrup complement each other perfectly, making this a true crowd-pleaser for any party."

GINGER SYRUP

1/2 cup filtered water

1/2 cup granulated maple sugar

1 (2-oz) piece of fresh ginger (about 4 inches)

SANGRIA

3 cups Pinot Grigio (nearly an entire 750-ml bottle)

6 oz spiced rum

6 oz Ginger Syrup (above)

6 oz fresh orange juice

3 oz fresh lemon juice

Fresh mint sprigs, for garnish (optional)

Orange slices, for garnish (optional)

To make the syrup, pour the water into a small saucepan over medium-low heat. Whisk in the sugar until dissolved. Peel and roughly chop the ginger, add it to the saucepan, and allow to simmer in the sugar syrup for 15 minutes. Pour the mixture into a blender and pulse to further incorporate the ginger. Allow to sit for 5–10 minutes, then strain the solids from the syrup.

To make the sangria, combine the wine, rum, ginger syrup, and citrus juices in a large pitcher. Add ice and stir to combine. Garnish with fresh mint sprigs and orange slices, if desired.

Cook's Note:

Adding a small amount of sparkling water to a glass of this sangria makes it extra-refreshing and fun!

savory things

cauliflower crust vegetable pizza

Yield: **1 large pizza**   Prep time: **40 minutes**   Cook time: **25 minutes**

• Nut-free

 "One of the foods people miss most when they go Paleo is pizza, and who could possibly blame them? There are many different grain-free options for pizza crusts; this particular recipe yields a thin-crust pizza. We love loading it up with fresh vegetables, and often add prosciutto or pepperoni to the mix as well. Given the effort required, we sometimes make a double batch so that we are sure to have leftovers! "

Pizza Sauce (pg 256)

1/2 head cauliflower, finely grated

1 cup (110 grams) arrowroot starch, plus up to 2 Tbsp more

1 heaping cup (62 grams) finely grated Parmesan cheese

1 large egg, beaten

1 tsp dried oregano

1/4 tsp ground black pepper

1/4 tsp garlic powder

1/4 tsp onion powder

TOPPINGS

1 Roma tomato, thinly sliced

1/2 cup sliced cremini mushrooms

1/2 red or green bell pepper, sliced

Small handful of fresh basil leaves

8 oz buffalo mozzarella, sliced (optional)

Make the Pizza Sauce. While the sauce is simmering, make the crust.

Place the grated cauliflower in a few layers of paper towel. Squeeze out as much liquid as possible and weigh (preferable for accuracy) or measure the cauliflower, shooting for 183 grams or 1 1/4 cups.

In a large mixing bowl, combine the cauliflower, 1 cup of the arrowroot starch, Parmesan cheese, egg, and spices. Use your hands to combine the mixture. Depending on how much water is left in the cauliflower and the atmospheric conditions, you may need to add a little more arrowroot starch: Begin by adding a teaspoon at a time, and continue to work the mixture with your hands until a cohesive dough forms.

Preheat the oven to 400°F. Liberally grease a metal baking sheet with duck fat, and shape the dough into a crust over the greased surface. Bake the crust for 12 minutes. The crust will look fully cooked, but not yet browned.

Remove the crust from the oven and bump up the oven temperature to 450°F. Top the crust with the sauce and toppings and return the pizza to the oven to bake for an additional 10–12 minutes, until the cheese (if using) has melted and the crust has golden brown edges.

fried wontons

Serves: **8**   Prep time: **20 minutes**   Cook time: **30 minutes**

· Dairy-free   · Nightshade-free

 66 Before my Paleo days, I used to love going out for Chinese food. One local restaurant served fried wontons, which are basically thin strips of dough that bubble and puff up to crispy perfection when fried. The day we finally nailed this recipe was one of our great triumphs in writing this book. This is a great dish to make in advance of dinner to set out as an appetizer, or to use as a garnish on our Asian Chicken Salad (pg 110). 99

Wrapper Dough (pg 336)

2 cups duck fat or other cooking fat of choice

Sea salt

Prepare the Wrapper Dough, then dust a sheet of parchment paper lightly with tapioca starch.

Place the ball of dough on the parchment and lightly press the dough down with your hands to flatten it.

Dust a rolling pin with tapioca starch and roll the dough into a very thin sheet, about 1/4–1/8 inch thick. You want the dough to be as thin as possible, while still being workable. Using a chef's knife or pizza cutter, slice the dough into 1-by-2-inch pieces.

In a deep, heavy saucepan, heat the duck fat to 350°F. We recommend monitoring the temperature using a candy thermometer. If you don't have a candy thermometer, you can test the temperature using a small piece of dough. Drop the dough in the hot fat; if it fries gently and forms bubbles without browning, then the temperature is correct for frying.

Carefully drop the strips of dough, one at a time, into the hot fat and fry for 2–3 minutes per side, until golden brown. Remove the fried wontons from the fat, sprinkle with salt to taste, and allow to drain and cool on a wire rack. Leftovers can be stored in a zip-top plastic bag for 2–3 days at room temperature.

Cook's Note:

If you can't eat nuts, you can use Nut-Free Pasta Dough (pg 328) instead of Wrapper Dough to make the wontons.

grain-free sandwich bread

Yield: **1 standard loaf**   Prep time: **20 minutes**   Cook time: **1 hour**

• Dairy-free

❝The blend of grain-free flours in this bread creates a flavor and texture similar to whole wheat bread. I love to enjoy this bread simply toasted with a healthy serving of salted butter on top, but it is also fantastic with sliced turkey, lettuce, and Homemade Mayonnaise (pg 244).❞

Palm shortening for greasing the pan

1 3/4 cups (159 grams) blanched almond flour

1/2 cup (56 grams) chestnut flour

1/2 cup (56 grams) potato starch

1/4 cup (27 grams) arrowroot starch

2 tsp baking powder, store-bought or homemade (pg 274)

1 tsp sea salt

1 cup full-fat coconut milk

4 large eggs, separated

1 Tbsp apple cider vinegar

1 Tbsp pure maple syrup

Preheat the oven to 350°F. Liberally grease a standard-size glass loaf pan with palm shortening. Trim a sheet of parchment paper to fit the length of the loaf pan, allowing for extra on the long sides to help you remove the loaf when finished. Set aside.

In a large mixing bowl, combine the almond flour, chestnut flour, potato starch, arrowroot starch, baking powder, and salt. In a medium-sized mixing bowl, combine the coconut milk, egg yolks, vinegar, and maple syrup and blend with an electric hand mixer until smooth. Pour the wet ingredients into the dry ingredients and blend with the hand mixer until smooth.

In a stand mixer or with the hand mixer, whip the egg whites until stiff peaks form. Carefully fold the egg whites into the batter.

Pour the batter into the prepared loaf pan. Bake on the middle rack of the oven for 1 hour, until a toothpick inserted comes out clean.

Remove from the oven and allow to cool completely before removing the bread from the pan. Slice and serve as desired. Keep refrigerated or freeze for later use.

Variation: Hamburger Buns

To make this recipe into burger buns, pour the batter into English muffin rings on a parchment-lined baking sheet. Bake in a preheated 350 °F oven for 40 minutes, or until a toothpick inserted comes out clean. Makes 6 buns.

nightshade-free pizza

Serves: **6**   Prep time: **30 minutes**   Cook time: **30–35 minutes**

• Dairy-free   • Nut-free   • Nightshade-free

Nut-Free Pesto (pg 268)

CRUST

2 1/2 cups (292 grams) tapioca starch, divided

1/3 cup (42 grams) coconut flour

1 Tbsp Baking Powder (pg 274)

1 tsp sea salt

1 tsp dried oregano

1/2 tsp garlic powder

1/2 tsp onion powder

1/2 tsp ground black pepper

4 large eggs, beaten

1/4 cup filtered water

3 Tbsp coconut oil, melted

TOPPINGS

2 cremini mushrooms, thinly sliced

1/4 cup baby arugula

3 slices prosciutto, torn apart

6 very thin slices red onion

8 oz buffalo mozzarella, sliced (optional; omit for dairy-free)

Prepare the pesto and set aside. Preheat the oven to 350°F and line a large baking sheet with parchment paper.

In a medium-sized mixing bowl, place 2 cups of the tapioca starch, coconut flour, baking powder, salt, oregano, garlic powder, onion powder, and pepper. Stir the dry ingredients with a spoon until they are evenly combined.

Create a small hole in the center of the flour mixture and pour the eggs into the hole. Pour in the water and slowly blend the eggs and water into the flour mixture. Add the melted coconut oil and blend again until the mixture starts to come together and resemble a dough.

Add the remaining 1/2 cup of tapioca starch and, using your hands, knead the starch into the dough. This will create the real dough texture you are looking for. Form the dough into a ball and place it on the parchment-lined baking sheet. Carefully form the dough into a pizza crust by pressing outward in a circle with your hands. Massaging a bit of coconut oil into your hands will help you keep a nice, smooth surface on the dough. Keep working with it until you have the shape you want; it should be about 3/8 inch thick, with slightly thicker edges.

Bake the crust for 20 minutes, until it is cooked through. Remove from the oven and increase the oven temperature to 450°F.

Cover the crust with a thin layer of the pesto and top with the mushrooms, baby arugula, prosciutto, onion, and buffalo mozzarella, if desired. Bake the pizza for 10 minutes, or 15 minutes if you added mozzarella.

nut-free pasta dough

Serves: **4**   Prep time: **30 minutes**   Cook time: **10 minutes**

· Dairy-free   · Nut-free   · Nightshade-free

 66I couldn't have successfully created this recipe without my dear friend Brittany Angell. She is one of the most talented gluten/grain-free bakers I know, and she helped me figure out how to make this nut-free version of Wrapper Dough (pg 336) so that people with nut allergies can enjoy Empanadas (pg 76), Pork Dumplings (pg 96), and Fried Wontons (pg 322), too. In the process of creating this dough, we found that it also makes fantastic pasta! 99

1 1/2 cups (179 grams) plus 2 Tbsp tapioca starch, divided

3 Tbsp (24 grams) coconut flour

1 tsp xanthan gum (see Notes)

1/2 tsp sea salt

1 large egg

1 large egg white

1/2 cup filtered water, room temperature

1/2 Tbsp palm shortening

Extra-virgin olive oil

In a medium-sized mixing bowl, combine 1 1/2 cups of the tapioca starch, coconut flour, xanthan gum, and salt. In a small mixing bowl, whisk together the egg and egg white until blended. Form a hole in the middle of the flour mixture, pour the whisked egg into the hole, and stir to combine. Pour the water over the mixture and stir to combine.

Knead the mixture with your hands. Once a dough has formed, knead the palm shortening into the dough until you have a smooth, well-formed ball. If the dough is still slightly sticky, dust it with the remaining 2 Tbsp of tapioca starch. The dough is now ready to be used as a nut-free option for making Empanadas, Pork Dumplings, or Fried Wontons. To make it into pasta, complete the steps below.

To create fettuccine noodles, divide the dough into thirds and flatten each portion with your hands. Dust a pasta maker with tapioca starch and run the dough through the roller on the wide setting once to prepare the dough to be cut into noodles. Once you have created a thin sheet of dough, liberally dust both sides of the dough with tapioca starch and run the dough through the fettuccine setting.

To cook the noodles, bring a large pot of salted water to a gentle boil. Drizzle olive oil on the surface of the water, carefully add the noodles, and boil for about 4 minutes, gently stirring to prevent the noodles from sticking together. Rinse under cold water and gently toss with olive oil or the pasta sauce of your choice to prevent them from sticking together.

Cook's Notes:

Xanthan gum is an ingredient we seldom cook with; however, it creates the elastic texture necessary for making pasta with coconut flour. It is known to cause digestive distress in individuals who have gut sensitivities. If you cannot tolerate it, you can use Wrapper Dough (pg 336) to make these noodles. If you are not planning to use the dough immediately, wrap it tightly in plastic wrap and place it in the fridge to keep it from drying out.

quiche crust

Yield: **one 9-inch crust**   Prep time: **15 minutes**   Cook time: **15 minutes**

• Dairy-free   • Nightshade-free

1 1/4 cups (125 grams) blanched almond flour

2/3 cup (75 grams) tapioca starch

1 tsp garlic powder

1 tsp onion powder

1 tsp dried oregano

1 tsp sea salt

1/2 tsp ground black pepper

2 large eggs

1 Tbsp coconut oil, melted

Preheat the oven to 325°F.

In a medium-sized mixing bowl, combine the almond flour, tapioca starch, garlic powder, onion powder, oregano, salt, and pepper.

In a small bowl, whisk the eggs until frothy. Add the eggs to the flour mixture and stir to combine. Add the melted coconut oil and knead it into the dough using your hands.

Carefully press the dough into a 9-inch pie pan or tart pan until you have a thin, even layer of crust over the entire pan. Bake on the middle rack of the oven for 15 minutes. Let the crust cool slightly before filling.

savory chestnut flour pie crusts

Yield: **4 single-serving crusts with tops or one 9-inch crust**   Prep time: **10 minutes**   Cook time: **22–25 minutes**

• Dairy-free   • Nightshade-free

1 cup (119 grams) chestnut flour

2/3 cup (81 grams) plus 1 Tbsp arrowroot starch, divided

1 tsp sea salt

1 tsp ground black pepper

1 tsp dried oregano

1/2 tsp garlic powder

2 large eggs

1/2 cup palm shortening, divided

Preheat the oven to 350°F.

In a medium-sized mixing bowl, combine the chestnut flour, 2/3 cup of the arrowroot starch, salt, pepper, oregano, and garlic powder.

In a small mixing bowl, whisk the eggs until frothy. Pour the whisked eggs into the flour mixture and stir to combine. Add 1/4 cup of the palm shortening and knead it into the dough. Once the 1/4 cup of shortening is completely incorporated, knead the remaining 1/4 cup of shortening into the dough.

Sprinkle the remaining 1 Tbsp of arrowroot starch over the dough and knead again to combine. Roll out the dough between two sheets of parchment paper to a thickness of 1/8 inch. If using mini pie pans, use the pie cutter included in the kit to cut the correct size for the pie pan, including the top layer of crust. Press the bottom layer of dough into the pie pan, and reserve the tops for after the filling is added.

Bake the crusts for 10 minutes, until cooked through (see Notes). Remove from the oven and allow to cool slightly, then fill with our Scottish Meat Pie filling (pg 104) or the savory filling of your choice. Top with a second layer of crust, if desired, carefully attaching the top layer by wetting the rim of the crust and lightly pressing together, and bake for an additional 12–15 minutes.

Cook's Notes:

We used a Chicago Metallic Pot Pie Pan set to create these personal-sized pie crusts. That kit comes with the pan and the tools to cut the crusts for the bottom and top. Alternatively, you can use four 5-inch mini pie pans to create crusts of the same size, or use a standard 9-inch pie pan to make one pie. For a 9-inch crust, the total cook time will be 15–20 minutes.

This crust can also be used to make a chicken pot pie or minced meat pie.

tortillas

Yield: **8–10 tortillas**   Prep time: **5 minutes**   Cook time: **20 minutes**

· Dairy-free   · Nut-free   · Nightshade-free

5 large eggs

3/4 cup full-fat coconut milk

1/4 cup (32 grams) coconut flour

1/4 cup (27 grams) arrowroot starch

1/2 tsp sea salt

6 grinds black pepper

8 tsp ghee, store-bought or homemade (pg 286), or other cooking fat of choice, divided

In a medium-sized mixing bowl, blend the eggs with the coconut milk with an electric hand mixer until frothy. Add the coconut flour and blend again until combined. Add the arrowroot starch, salt, and pepper and blend again until the batter is completely smooth.

Heat 2 tsp of the ghee in a 9 1/2-inch stainless-steel skillet over medium heat. Swirl the skillet so that the ghee coats the bottom evenly. If the ghee starts to smoke, turn the temperature down to just below medium. The skillet should be hot enough to cook the tortillas, but not so hot that you can't get the batter to coat the bottom of the skillet in a thin, even layer.

Beat the batter once more before frying to ensure that it is freshly blended. Using a measuring cup, scoop a scant 1/4 cup of batter. Lift the skillet from the burner slightly and tilt it toward the cup of batter in your opposite hand. Pour the batter into the center of the skillet and carefully rotate the skillet with your wrist so that the batter covers the bottom of the skillet in a thin layer, like a crepe.

Place the skillet back down on the burner and cook for 60 seconds, or until the edges start to lift and the bottom is lightly browned. Using a small spatula, carefully lift the edges all around the tortilla to make sure that nothing is sticking, slide the spatula under the tortilla, and flip. Cook the tortilla on the opposite side for 30–60 seconds, until lightly browned like a classic corn tortilla. Repeat until you have used all of the batter.

wrapper dough

Serves: **4**   Time needed: **10 minutes**

· Dairy-free   · Nightshade-free

 66This versatile, multipurpose dough is used in many recipes in this book. You can use it to make Empanadas (pg 76), Pork Dumplings (pg 96), or Fried Wontons (pg 322). It can also be used in place of the Cappello's lasagna sheets in our Pork and Apple Ravioli recipe (pg 92). 99

1 cup (113 grams) blanched almond flour

1 1/4 cups (146 grams) tapioca starch

1/2 tsp sea salt

1 large egg, whisked

1/4 cup filtered water

1 tsp coconut oil, melted

Combine the almond flour, tapioca starch, and salt in a small mixing bowl. Add the whisked egg and water and stir to combine. Add the melted coconut oil and knead until you have a smooth, round ball of dough.

Use the dough immediately or refrigerate until ready to use. It can be frozen as well.

Cook's Note:

If you can't eat nuts, you can use Nut-Free Pasta Dough (pg 328) in place of Wrapper Dough.

zucchini fritters

Serves: **6–8 as an appetizer; makes fifteen to twenty 2-inch fritters**   Prep time: **15 minutes**   Cook time: **15 minutes**

· Dairy-free   · Nut-free   · Nightshade-free

"Sometimes recipes spring forth from happy accidents. One day I was fooling around with ingredients, trying to mix up a savory funnel cake batter. I was a little off for that sort of result, but I ended up with a fantastic fritter! It just goes to show that you should experiment in the kitchen once in a while. Don't be afraid to mess things up, because the results might surprise you!"

1/3 cup finely shredded zucchini (avoid seeds)

1 cup (110 grams) arrowroot starch

2 large eggs, beaten

1 Tbsp sparkling water

1/4 tsp sea salt, plus more for sprinkling

1/4 tsp ground black pepper

1/4 tsp ground turmeric

2 to 3 cups Rendered Lard (pg 294), duck fat, or coconut oil, for frying

Place the shredded zucchini in a clean kitchen towel or paper towel and squeeze out as much water as possible.

In a medium-sized mixing bowl, stir together the arrowroot starch, eggs, and sparkling water. Add the salt, pepper, and turmeric, then gently stir in the zucchini.

Heat the lard in a deep, heavy saucepan to 375°F, using a candy thermometer to monitor the temperature. The wider your pan, the more fat you will need. Try to get 3/4–1 inch of fat in the pan.

Use a large soup spoon (or heaping tablespoon) to carefully drop spoonfuls of the batter into the hot fat. Do not crowd the fritters, as this will alter the fat temperature. Fry the fritters for 2–3 minutes per side, until golden brown. Remove from the fat and allow to drain on a wire rack set over a rimmed baking sheet to catch drips, or a plate lined with a paper towel. While still hot, sprinkle with a small amount of salt. Repeat with the rest of the batter, allowing the fat to come back up to temperature between batches.

sweet things

apple streusel muffins

Yield: **15 mini muffins**   Prep time: **15 minutes**   Cook time: **30 minutes**

· Dairy-free   · Nightshade-free

1/4 cup (28 grams) chestnut flour

1/4 cup (32 grams) coconut flour

2 Tbsp granulated maple sugar

2 tsp Baking Powder (pg 274)

1/2 tsp ground cinnamon

1/2 tsp sea salt

5 large eggs

1 tsp pure vanilla extract

1/2 cup palm shortening, melted

1 medium red apple, shredded

TOPPING

2 Tbsp blanched almond flour

1 Tbsp coconut sugar

1/4 tsp ground cinnamon

1/4 tsp ground nutmeg

Preheat the oven to 350°F. Line 15 wells of a mini muffin tin with mini muffin papers.

In a medium-sized mixing bowl, stir together the chestnut flour, coconut flour, maple sugar, baking powder, cinnamon, and salt until blended. In a small mixing bowl, use an electric hand mixer to blend the eggs and vanilla extract. Add the wet ingredients to the dry ingredients and blend with the hand mixer until smooth. Add the melted palm shortening and blend again until smooth.

Place the shredded apple in a clean kitchen towel or paper towel and wring it with your hands to squeeze out as much liquid as possible. Add the shredded apple to the batter and blend again with the hand mixer.

In a small bowl, combine the topping ingredients.

Using a small cookie scoop, scoop some batter into each mini muffin cup. Spoon a small amount of the topping mixture (about 1/2 tsp) onto each muffin. Bake for 30 minutes, or until a toothpick inserted comes out clean.

Allow the muffins to cool slightly before serving. (We like these with grass-fed butter.) Keep any leftover muffins in a tightly sealed container in the fridge for up to 1 week.

berry and ginger granita

Serves: **8**   Prep time: **20 minutes**   Cook time: **10 minutes**   Freeze time: **4–5 hours**

· Dairy-free   · Nut-free   · Egg-free   · Nightshade-free

1 cup filtered water

1/3 cup granulated maple sugar

2 tsp grated fresh ginger

2 cups diced strawberries

1 cup fresh raspberries

Juice of 1 lemon (3 Tbsp)

Juice of 1 lime (2 Tbsp)

Mint leaves or citrus fruits, for garnish (optional)

In a small saucepan over medium-high heat, combine the water and maple sugar. Bring the mixture to a boil and stir to fully dissolve the sugar. Remove from the heat and add the ginger. Allow to cool to room temperature, then place in the refrigerator to chill the syrup.

While the ginger syrup is chilling, make the berry coulis: Place the strawberries, raspberries, and citrus juices in a large, wide-mouth mason jar. Blend with an immersion blender until smooth.

Pour the blended fruit through a fine-mesh strainer set over a bowl, and work the pulp around until all of the juice has run through the strainer into the bowl below. Discard the pulp and repeat with any remaining fruit. What should remain is a velvety fruit juice without any pulp or seeds.

Once the ginger syrup has cooled, pour it into the fruit juice and stir to combine. Pour the fruit juice mixture into a 9-by-9-inch casserole dish or other similar-size shallow dish. Place the dish in the freezer and rake the granita every hour or so with a fork. Once ice crystals have formed, allow the mixture to freeze for a few hours without disturbing it.

To serve, use a fork or spoon to "shave" the ice into serving bowls. Garnish with mint leaves or citrus fruits, if desired, and serve immediately.

blueberry tart

Yield: **one 9-inch pie**   Prep time: **15 minutes**   Cook time: **20 minutes**   Chill time: **2 hours**

· Dairy-free   · Nut-free   · Nightshade-free

1 Nut-Free Pie/Tart Crust (pg 386)

BLUEBERRY FILLING

5 cups fresh blueberries, divided

3/4 cup granulated maple sugar

3 Tbsp arrowroot starch

1/4 cup cold filtered water

Pinch of sea salt

Juice of 1/2 lemon (1 1/2 Tbsp)

1 1/2 tsp ghee, store-bought or homemade (pg 286)

Fresh mint, for garnish (optional)

Prepare the crust using a 9-inch pie pan or tart pan.

Rinse the blueberries and set aside to dry. In a medium-sized saucepan, whisk together the maple sugar, arrowroot starch, and cold water. Add the salt and lemon juice and whisk to combine.

Warm the mixture over medium heat, whisking continuously for 1 minute. Add 3 cups of the fresh blueberries and cook, stirring frequently, until the mixture starts to bubble and the blueberries start to pop, 3–5 minutes. Continue to cook, stirring often, until the texture starts to resemble that of blueberry jam and the liquid has thickened and started to gel slightly.

Remove the pan from the heat and stir in the remaining 2 cups of blueberries and the ghee. Pour the blueberry filling into the prebaked crust and refrigerate until set, at least 2 hours. Garnish with fresh mint, if desired, and serve.

chocolate chip sunbutter cookies

Yield: **22 cookies**   Prep time: **15 minutes**   Cook time: **30 minutes**

· Dairy-free   · Nut-free   · Nightshade-free

1 cup sunflower seed butter

2 large eggs

1 tsp pure vanilla extract

1/4 tsp sea salt

2/3 cup granulated maple sugar

2 1/2 Tbsp coconut flour

1/2 tsp Baking Powder (pg 274)

1 Tbsp palm shortening, gently melted

1/3 cup allergen-free dark chocolate chips

Preheat the oven to 350°F. Line two baking sheets with parchment paper.

In a medium-sized mixing bowl, combine the sunflower seed butter, eggs, vanilla extract, and salt. Blend with an electric hand mixer until smooth.

Sift in the maple sugar, coconut flour, and baking powder and blend until smooth. Add the melted palm shortening and blend again until smooth.

Stir in the chocolate chips. Using a #50 cookie scoop or two spoons, scoop 1 1/4 Tbsp-sized portions of the dough onto the lined baking sheets, keeping in mind that the cookies will spread about 1/2 inch. Lightly press down on the cookies with your hand to flatten them slightly.

Bake each sheet of cookies on the center rack of the oven for 15 minutes, until they are cooked through with golden edges. Let cool on a wire rack before serving. The cookies will keep for up to 1 week in a tightly sealed container in the refrigerator.

Cook's Notes:

Baking soda is known to turn sunflower seeds green when cooked. Luckily, baking powder does not, due to the acidity from the cream of tartar. You can use baking powder in any recipe that calls for sunflower seeds or sunflower seed butter, and your baked goods will keep their color and rise nicely!

You can make ice cream sandwiches with these cookies by using Maple Vanilla Bean Ice Cream (pg 380).

chocolate-covered bacon

Serves: **4**   Prep time: **10 minutes**   Cook time: **20 minutes**   Chill time: **20 minutes**

· Dairy-free   · Nut-free   · Egg-free   · Nightshade-free

"In the world of Paleo indulgences, it doesn't get much better than chocolate or bacon. But chocolate *and* bacon? This combination might sound odd at first, but the flavor is mostly sweet, with the smokiness and saltiness of bacon layered in. I especially like the extra little hint of cinnamon on top. If you have a Bill-sized sweet tooth (that is, a big one), you should probably plan to make extra."

6 strips bacon (see Note)

1/2 cup allergen-free dark chocolate chips

1 Tbsp ground cinnamon

1 Tbsp granulated maple sugar

Preheat the oven to 400°F. Cut the bacon into 2-inch pieces. Bake the bacon on a rack set over a rimmed baking sheet for 15–20 minutes. Remove the bacon from the oven and place it on a paper towel to cool for 5–10 minutes.

In a metal bowl set over a pot of water on medium-low heat, melt the chocolate, stirring continuously. Using a fork or slotted spatula, dip the baked bacon in the chocolate, then set on a rack over a paper towel to catch the drips. Using a spoon, drizzle more chocolate over the coated bacon to create a pretty texture. Place in the freezer to set for 20 minutes.

Mix together the cinnamon and maple sugar, then place the mixture in a small fine-mesh sieve. Evenly dust the chilled coated bacon with the cinnamon sugar by tapping the side of the sieve with your palm.

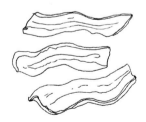

Cook's Note:

If you are following a nightshade-free diet, use care to select bacon that does not contain nightshades in the spice mixture. Alternately, you can follow our recipe for curing your own bacon on pg 280.

chocolate fruit and nut bars

Serves: **8–10**   Prep time: **30 minutes**   Chill time: **1 hour**

· Dairy-free   · Egg-free   · Nightshade-free

2 oz (4 squares) bittersweet chocolate

1 1/2 Tbsp coconut oil

1/2 tsp pure vanilla extract

1/2 cup raw almonds

1/2 cup unsweetened shredded coconut

1/4 cup allergen-free semisweet chocolate chips

1/4 tsp sea salt

1 1/2 cups Medjool dates, pitted

Line a standard-size loaf pan with plastic wrap, with extra length on one side for covering the pan later, and set aside.

In a double boiler or small saucepan, melt the chocolate and coconut oil over medium-low to low heat, stirring continuously. If you are not using a double boiler, be sure to melt the chocolate and oil over low heat, and stir to prevent the chocolate from burning. Once the chocolate and oil are melted and combined, remove from the heat and stir in the vanilla extract.

In a food processor, pulse the almonds until roughly chopped. Make sure that there are no large pieces remaining, but it should be a rough chop, not a fine chop. Pour the chopped almonds into a mixing bowl. Add the coconut, chocolate chips, and salt and stir to combine.

Add the dates to the food processor and process on high speed until you have created a paste. The dates may form a ball in the food processor, and that's fine.

Scoop the cooled chocolate and oil mixture into the food processor and push the dates down. Process again on high speed until the chocolate and oil are combined with the dates. Add the almond mixture to the food processor and pulse to combine slightly.

Pour the date mixture back into the mixing bowl and knead it with your hands until it is fully combined. Press the mixture evenly into the lined loaf pan. Lightly cover the top with the excess plastic wrap and place the pan in the fridge to set for 1 hour.

After 1 hour, remove the pan from the fridge and carefully pull out the date mixture using the excess plastic wrap as handles. Place the mixture on a cutting board and cut into bars. Keep refrigerated in a tightly sealed container for up to 2 weeks, or freeze for longer storage.

Cook's Note:

These bars can also be cut into bite-sized squares or made into 1-oz balls.

chocolate "peanut butter" squares

Yields: **24 squares**   Prep time: **30 minutes**   Chill time: **40 minutes**

• Dairy-free   • Egg-free   • Nightshade-free

 " These bars are just like the ones my mom used to make for us when I was a kid. I can still picture that big rectangular Tupperware container sitting on the counter, filled to the top with these (with layers of wax paper between). This vivid memory is no coincidence, because I absolutely loved this treat. Thankfully, Hayley's re-creation is just like the real deal. "

1 cup raw cashews (see Note)

1 cup unsweetened shredded coconut

1/4 cup pure maple syrup

1 Tbsp coconut oil

1 tsp pure vanilla extract

1/2 tsp sea salt

1 cup sunflower seed butter

20 oz allergen-free dark chocolate chips

Pulse the cashews in a food processor until finely chopped. Add the coconut, maple syrup, coconut oil, and vanilla extract and pulse again to combine with the cashews.

Add the salt and sunflower seed butter to the food processor and pulse again until a ball of dough has formed. Press the dough in an even layer into a 9-by-13-inch baking dish and place in the refrigerator to chill while you melt the chocolate.

In a double boiler or small saucepan over medium-low heat, melt the chocolate chips, stirring frequently. If you are not using a double boiler, be sure to melt the chocolate over very low heat, and stir constantly to prevent it from burning. Once the chocolate is completely melted, remove the dough from the fridge, pour the melted chocolate over the top, and spread it with a spatula to evenly coat the base. Place the dish in the freezer to set, about 40 minutes.

Allow the bars to defrost a bit before slicing them into 2-inch squares. Keep refrigerated until ready to serve. These will keep for 1–2 weeks in the fridge, or you can freeze them for longer storage.

Cook's Note:

To make this recipe completely nut-free, substitute sunflower seeds for the cashews.

chocolate pudding pie

Yield: **one 9-inch pie**   Prep time: **15 minutes**   Cook time: **30 minutes**   Chill time: **2 hours**

• Dairy-free   • Nightshade-free

1 Graham Cracker Pie/Tart Crust (pg 386)

CHOCOLATE PUDDING FILLING

3 cups full-fat coconut milk, divided

1/2 cup allergen-free semi-sweet chocolate chips

1/3 cup granulated maple sugar

3 Tbsp cocoa powder

3 large egg yolks

1/4 cup arrowroot starch

1 tsp pure vanilla extract

1/4 tsp sea salt

Whipped Coconut Cream (pg 398) or whipped heavy cream (if dairy is tolerated), for topping

Prepare the crust using a 9-inch pie pan or tart pan.

In a medium-sized saucepan over medium-low heat, combine 2 cups of the coconut milk with the chocolate chips, maple sugar, and cocoa powder. Whisk frequently until the chocolate chips have melted into the coconut milk. Raise the heat to medium to scald it; the mixture should just start to steam. Remove from the heat and set aside.

In a large mixing bowl, combine the remaining 1 cup of coconut milk with the egg yolks, arrowroot starch, vanilla extract, and salt. Whisk together until evenly combined.

Gradually whisk the scalded chocolate mixture, a little bit at a time, into the egg yolk mixture. Once fully combined, return the pudding mixture to the saucepan. Heat over medium heat, whisking constantly. As it approaches a bubble, it will thicken. Whisk at this temperature for another 30–60 seconds, then remove from the heat. Immediately pour the mixture into the prepared crust.

Allow the pie to cool slightly, then refrigerate until set, about 2 hours. Serve topped with Whipped Coconut Cream.

Cook's Note:

To make this pie completely nut-free, use the Nut-Free Pie/Tart Crust on pg 386 in place of the Graham Cracker Pie/Tart Crust.

chocolate sunbutter cups

Yield: **24 mini cups**   Prep time: **15 minutes**   Chill time: **20 minutes**

· Dairy-free   · Nut-free   · Egg-free   · Nightshade-free

❝My self-control is always tested when I'm around Reese's Peanut Butter Cups. The amazing flavor combination of chocolate and peanut butter is one of my all-time favorites. These cups are a whole lot better for you than store-bought candy, as the ingredients are all 'real food.' The little sprinkle of salt on top is my favorite part of this recipe—it's a nice touch to create the perfect salty and sweet balance. ❞

3 cups allergen-free dark chocolate chips

2 Tbsp coconut oil

1/2 cup sunflower seed butter

1 Tbsp granulated maple sugar

1 tsp pure vanilla extract

Coarse sea salt

Line a mini muffin tin with mini muffin papers.

In a small saucepan or double boiler over low heat, melt the chocolate chips and coconut oil, stirring. If you are not using a double boiler, be sure to melt the chocolate and oil over low heat, and stir to prevent the chocolate from burning. Once melted, remove from the heat and pour the melted chocolate into the mini muffin papers, filling each cup halfway. (The remaining chocolate will be used for the top layer.) Place the muffin tin in the freezer for about 10 minutes to firm up the chocolate.

While the chocolate is cooling, combine the sunflower seed butter, maple sugar, and vanilla extract in a small mixing bowl and mix together thoroughly. Remove the muffin tin from the freezer and spoon a small amount of the sunflower seed butter mixture into each cup. Cover with the remaining melted chocolate and place in the freezer for 2–3 minutes to set.

Sprinkle the top of each cup with coarse sea salt and return the muffin tin to the freezer until the chocolate is completely solid, about 20 minutes. These can be kept frozen until you're ready to enjoy them.

cranberry hand pies

Yield: **8 hand pies**   Prep time: **35 minutes**   Cook time: **30 minutes**

· Dairy-free   · Nightshade-free

3/4 cup Spiced Cranberry Relish (pg 224)

1/2 cup (75 grams) granulated maple sugar

1 1/2 cups (136 grams) blanched almond flour

1 1/2 cups (156 grams) arrowroot starch, plus more for dusting

1/2 tsp sea salt

1/4 tsp baking soda

3 Tbsp palm shortening

2 large egg whites, yolks reserved

1 large egg, whisked

Cook's Notes:

If you are making these pies in advance of a holiday gathering, we recommend making them one day ahead. Keep them tightly sealed in the fridge and warm them in the oven before serving.

Almond flour releases oil on its own, so the more you knead the dough, the more elastic it will become. If your dough is too crumbly even after this step, add 1 tsp of cold water at a time until you have a smooth ball of dough that can be rolled out easily.

For a fun alternative, use Blueberry Tart filling (pg 346) in place of the relish!

Prepare the cranberry relish and set aside.

Preheat the oven to 350°F, and line a baking sheet with parchment paper.

In a large mixing bowl, sift together the maple sugar, almond flour, arrowroot starch, salt, and baking soda. Using your hands, work the palm shortening into the flour mixture. Once the shortening is blended with the flour, you will have crumbly dough. Lightly whisk the egg whites and add them to the dough, using your hands to incorporate, until you have a smooth, nicely formed ball of dough. Add 1–2 Tbsp of arrowroot starch to the outside of the dough if it's a touch too sticky so that it can be easily rolled out into a thin layer.

Place a sheet of parchment paper on a flat surface large enough to roll the dough, and dust with arrowroot starch. Add half of the dough to the parchment and place another sheet of parchment on top of the dough. Roll out the dough to 1/8-inch thickness. Using the rim of a large, wide-mouth mason jar lid or an English muffin ring, cut out circles of dough, removing the extra dough around the outside.

Gently transfer the circles to the prepared baking sheet, placing them an inch or two apart. Repeat this process to create the tops of the pies.

Spoon a heaping tablespoon of the relish onto each circle of dough. Using your finger, run a rim of the reserved egg yolk around the outer edge of the crust so that the top layer sticks well.

Gently place the top circle of crust over the bottom circle with the relish and press the edges together with your fingers. Using a paring knife, create three slits in the top of each pie. Using a fork, press the edges again to create a pretty texture on the outside rim.

Lightly brush the tops of the pies with the whisked egg. Bake on the middle rack of the oven for 17 minutes. Remove the pies from the oven, turn up the oven temperature up to 375°F, and move the oven rack up one notch. Brush the pies once more with the egg wash, sprinkle with additional maple sugar, and bake for 5 more minutes. Allow the pies to cool on a wire rack before serving.

dairy-free chocolate mousse

Serves: **4**   Time needed: **10 minutes**

· Dairy-free   · Nut-free   · Egg-free   · Nightshade-free

"This mousse is the perfect dessert when you need a bit of decadence without any guilt. With just the slightest hint of banana flavor, this light and fluffy chocolate treat is sure to wow your taste buds."

2 ripe avocados, pitted and peeled

1 semi-ripe banana

1/4 cup pure maple syrup

2 Tbsp coconut sugar

2 tsp pure vanilla extract

1/4 tsp sea salt

1/2 cup cocoa powder

Fresh berries and mint leaves, for garnish

In a food processor or high-speed blender, purée the avocados, banana, and maple syrup on high speed until smooth.

Add the coconut sugar, vanilla extract, and salt and blend again until combined.

Add the cocoa powder and purée again until the mixture is smooth and fluffy and has turned a dark chocolate brown.

Serve immediately or chilled, garnished with fresh berries and mint leaves.

Cook's Note:

For a fancy presentation, as shown, scoop the mousse into a piping bag and use a Wilton 1M tip to pipe it into the serving cups.

dark chocolate, olive oil, and sea salt ice cream

Serves: **6**   Prep time: **15 minutes, plus 30 minutes to cool**   Processing time: **20 minutes**

· Dairy-free   · Nut-free   · Egg-free   · Nightshade-free

2 (13 1/2-oz) cans full-fat coconut milk

1/2 cup granulated maple sugar

1/3 cup cocoa powder

2 tsp pure vanilla extract

1 Tbsp grass-fed gelatin (see Notes)

1 1/2 tsp extra-virgin olive oil

1 tsp sea salt

Coarse sea salt, for garnish (optional)

Special equipment:

Ice cream maker

In a medium-sized saucepan, combine the coconut milk, maple sugar, cocoa powder, and vanilla extract. Pour the gelatin into a small bowl, which will allow you to better control the rate at which you incorporate it into the mixture.

Warm the coconut milk mixture over medium heat, whisking, until the sugar and cocoa powder have dissolved. Once the mixture starts to bubble slightly, reduce the heat to low. At this point, the mixture should stop bubbling and only have steam rising from it.

Very slowly sprinkle in the gelatin, whisking vigorously. This will allow the gelatin to fully dissolve into the hot milk. If you add the gelatin too quickly or don't whisk enough, it will create clumps.

Strain the mixture through a fine-mesh strainer into a glass mixing bowl. Allow to cool to room temperature, about 30 minutes.

Churn the chilled ice cream base in an ice cream maker according to the manufacturer's instructions. This should take about 20 minutes. Two minutes before the ice cream has finished churning, add the olive oil and sea salt. Enjoy immediately for a soft-serve like texture, or place in the freezer for 2 hours to harden before serving. Sprinkle with coarse sea salt, if desired.

Cook's Notes:

If you can't find grass-fed gelatin, you can substitute 1/4 cup of tapioca starch or arrowroot starch, but whisk it into the cold coconut milk mixture before heating it on the stovetop.

For a basic dark chocolate ice cream, simply omit the olive oil and sea salt from this recipe.

double chocolate chip cookies

Yield: **20 cookies**   Prep time: **15 minutes**   Cook time: **30 minutes**

• Dairy-free   • Nightshade-free

1 1/2 cups (139 grams) blanched almond flour

1/4 cup (18 grams) cocoa powder

1 tsp Baking Powder (pg 274)

1/2 tsp sea salt

2 large eggs

1/4 cup pure maple syrup

1 tsp pure vanilla extract

1/4 cup palm shortening

3/4 cup allergen-free dark chocolate chips

Preheat the oven to 375°F. Line two baking sheets with parchment paper.

In a medium-sized mixing bowl, combine the almond flour, cocoa powder, baking powder, and salt. Stir together until evenly blended.

In a separate mixing bowl, whisk together the eggs, maple syrup, and vanilla extract until smooth. Add the dry ingredients and the palm shortening and blend with an electric hand mixer until the batter is smooth. Fold in the chocolate chips.

Using a #50 cookie scoop or 2 spoons, drop 1 1/4 Tbsp-sized amounts of cookie dough onto the lined baking sheets. Smooth the tops of the cookies slightly with the scoop or a spoon for best results. Bake each sheet on the middle rack of the oven for 15 minutes, then allow to cool on a wire rack.

Cook's Note:

Serve with a chilled glass of nut milk (pg 300), if desired.

fluffy dairy-free chocolate frosting

Yield: **2 cups**   Prep time: **15 minutes**   Chill time: **1–2 hours**

• Dairy-free   • Nut-free   • Egg-free   • Nightshade-free

1 (13 1/2-oz) can full-fat coconut milk, refrigerated overnight (8-10 hours)

1 1/2 cups allergen-free semi-sweet chocolate chips

1 tsp pure vanilla extract

Open the can of coconut milk from the bottom and discard the water. Scoop 1/2 cup of the cream into a small saucepan over medium heat. Whisk the cream until smooth and heat it until scalding—steam rising from the cream, but not boiling.

Pour the chocolate chips into a small metal mixing bowl. Add the vanilla extract. Pour in the hot cream and whisk until the chocolate is completely melted and you have a thick, creamy chocolate mixture. Place the bowl in the fridge until the chocolate mixture is completely chilled, 1–2 hours.

Remove the chilled chocolate mixture from the fridge and whip it with an electric hand mixer on high speed until fluffy and lightened in color. Use immediately or refrigerate until ready to use. Before using refrigerated frosting, whip again to soften it and make sure it is fluffy.

Keep this frosting in a tightly sealed container in the fridge for up to 1 week, or freeze for longer storage.

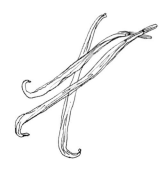

grain-free fudgy brownies

Yield: **24 brownies**   Prep time: **25 minutes**   Cook time: **30–35 minutes**

• Dairy-free   • Nightshade-free

❝Grain-free brownies tend to be too cakelike, crumbly, or dry, but these fudgy brownies will wow you with their perfect texture and flavor. You would never know that these moist, chocolaty brownies are completely free of grain.❞

6 oz (12 squares) dark chocolate

1/2 cup palm shortening, plus more for the baking dish

3/4 cup coconut sugar

1 tsp pure vanilla extract

1/2 cup (50 grams) chestnut flour

1 tsp Baking Powder, (pg 274)

1/2 tsp sea salt

4 large eggs

1/3 cup allergen-free dark chocolate chips (optional)

Shown with Fluffy Dairy-Free Chocolate Frosting (pg 368)

Preheat the oven to 350°F. Grease a 9-by-13-inch glass baking dish with palm shortening and line it with parchment paper for easy removal of the brownies.

Melt the dark chocolate and palm shortening in a small saucepan over medium-low heat, stirring frequently. Add the coconut sugar and vanilla extract and stir until smooth. Remove the pan from the heat and allow the chocolate mixture to cool slightly.

In a separate bowl, blend together the chestnut flour, baking powder, salt, and eggs. Once the chocolate mixture is tepid, pour it into the flour mixture and blend until smooth.

Pour the batter into the prepared baking dish. Sprinkle the top of the brownies with the chocolate chips before baking, if desired. Bake for 30–35 minutes, until a toothpick inserted comes out clean. Allow the brownies to cool completely in the pan, then cut into 2-inch squares and serve.

Keep these brownies in a tightly sealed container in the fridge for up to 1 week, or freeze, unfrosted, for longer storage.

granola two ways

Yield: **about 8 cups** Prep time: **30 minutes, plus 8 hours to soak** Dehydrating time: **10–12 hours**

· Dairy-free · Egg-free · Nightshade-free

2 cups raw slivered almonds

2 cups raw walnuts, roughly chopped

1 cup raw pecans, roughly chopped

1 cup raw pumpkin seeds

3/4 cup raw sunflower seeds

Filtered water

Pinch of sea salt

2/3 cup raw honey

1/4 cup coconut oil

CHOCOLATE COCONUT GRANOLA

2/3 cup allergen-free dark chocolate chips or chopped chocolate chunks

1/3 cup unsweetened shredded coconut

1 Tbsp pure vanilla extract

1/2 tsp sea salt

CINNAMON RAISIN GRANOLA

1 cup raisins

1 Tbsp pure vanilla extract

1/2 tsp sea salt

1/2 tsp ground cinnamon

1/4 tsp ground nutmeg

Combine the almonds, walnuts, pecans, pumpkin seeds, and sunflower seeds in a medium-sized mixing bowl. Cover with filtered water and add the salt. Cover the bowl with a towel or plastic wrap and let soak for 8 hours.

After 8 hours, drain the nuts and seeds and rinse them with fresh water. Divide the nuts and seeds equally between two large mixing bowls.

In a small saucepan, melt the honey and coconut oil over medium-low heat and stir to combine.

Make the Chocolate Coconut Granola: To one of the bowls of nuts and seeds, add the chocolate chips, coconut, vanilla extract, and salt and mix to combine.

Make the Cinnamon Raisin Granola: To the other bowl of nuts and seeds, add the raisins, vanilla extract, salt, cinnamon, and nutmeg and mix to combine.

Dress both bowls equally with the honey and coconut oil mixture and stir to combine with the nuts and seeds.

If using a food dehydrator, spread the granola evenly over the dehydrator sheet and dehydrate per the manufacturer's instructions for 10–12 hours. If using the oven, preheat the oven to 110°F. Spread the granola evenly over two parchment-lined baking sheets and dehydrate in the oven for 10–12 hours. If your oven does not go down to 110°F, put it on the lowest setting and keep the oven door ajar while dehydrating the granola.

Remove the granola from the dehydrator or oven and allow to cool. Store in a sealed container in the fridge or freezer until ready to serve. Enjoy it within 1 week, refrigerated, or keep this granola in the freezer for longer storage.

lemon blueberry waffles

Serves: **4**   Prep time: **10 minutes**   Cook time: **10 minutes**

· Dairy-free   · Nut-free   · Nightshade-free

❝When I think of waffles, I think of a leisurely brunch with family. Waffles are not a rushed breakfast—at least not when you make them from scratch. As with any Paleo meal, there's a reason to slow down and enjoy the process of cooking. We made these waffles for our family brunch on Mother's Day, and when I make them now, I always think of enjoying them with my family talking and laughing around the dining table. ❞

WAFFLES

6 large eggs

1/2 cup (55 grams) arrowroot starch

1/4 cup (32 grams) coconut flour

2 tsp Baking Powder (pg 274)

1 tsp coconut sugar

1/2 tsp sea salt

1/4 cup full-fat coconut milk

1 Tbsp grated lemon zest

1/2 cup fresh blueberries

TOPPINGS

Fresh blueberries

Pure maple syrup

Grass-fed butter (optional)

In a high-speed blender, combine the eggs, arrowroot starch, coconut flour, baking powder, coconut sugar, salt, coconut milk, and lemon zest and process until smooth. Stir in the blueberries by hand.

Heat a waffle iron to medium heat and grease the surface with coconut oil. Once the waffle iron is up to temperature, pour the batter onto the grids, using the waffle manufacturer's guidelines for suggested cup quantity. Be sure to ladle the batter evenly over the surface of the waffle iron, and cook for 2–3 minutes (the time and amount of batter will vary depending on your particular waffle iron). Repeat with the remaining batter.

Serve the waffles topped with more fresh blueberries, maple syrup, and some grass-fed butter, if desired.

lemon curd

Yield: **1 cup**   Prep time: **10 minutes**   Cook time: **10 minutes**   Chill time: **at least 1 hour**

• Nut-free   • Nightshade-free

❝Lemon curd is one of my favorite sweet treats. That's why it found its way between the layers of our wedding cake, and it was perfect for a hot August wedding. Lemon curd adds a fresh, sweet, and tangy flavor to baked goods. It's fantastic piped into cupcakes or simply drizzled over fresh berries.❞

7 large egg yolks

1 cup granulated maple sugar

Juice of 2 large lemons (1/3 cup)

Grated zest of 1 lemon

1/2 cup (1 stick) grass-fed butter, cubed

Special equipment:

Candy thermometer

Pour about 2 inches of filtered water into a small saucepan and bring to a simmer over medium-low heat.

While the water is heating, whisk together the egg yolks and maple sugar in a metal bowl. Once combined, whisk in the lemon juice and zest.

Place the metal bowl over the simmering water and whisk the mixture until it is thick and coats the back of a spoon, monitoring the temperature with a candy thermometer. The temperature of the mixture should reach 175°F.

Remove the bowl from the heat. Strain the mixture through a fine-mesh sieve into a large, wide-mouth mason jar and allow to cool to 145°F. Add the butter a cube at a time and blend until smooth using an immersion blender.

Once all of the butter is blended in, strain the mixture one more time. Place the curd in the refrigerator to chill for at least 1 hour. It will keep in the fridge for up to 1 week, tightly covered, or in the freezer for up to 3 months.

Cook's Note:

We use this lemon curd between the layers of the Wedding Cake (pg 396), and as the filling for Luscious Lemon Cupcakes (pg 378). You can also use lemon curd as your filling for miniature tarts, or simply spread it on a slice of grain-free toast. Since this curd keeps for a while, it can be made well in advance of other recipes that you plan to use it with.

luscious lemon cupcakes

Yield: **1 dozen standard or 24 mini cupcakes**   Prep time: **15 minutes**   Cook time: **20 minutes**

• Nut-free   • Nightshade-free

Lemon Curd (pg 376), for filling

Vanilla Buttercream Frosting (pg 394)

3/4 cup arrowroot starch

1/2 cup coconut flour

1/2 tsp sea salt

1/4 tsp baking soda

6 large eggs

1/2 cup pure maple syrup

2 tsp pure vanilla extract

1/4 cup palm shortening

Special equipment:

Piping bags and piping tips

Make the lemon curd and place in the refrigerator to chill. While the curd is chilling, make the frosting and set aside until needed.

Preheat the oven to 350°F. Line a standard muffin tin or mini muffin tin with cupcake papers.

In a large mixing bowl, stir together the arrowroot starch, coconut flour, salt, and baking soda until blended. In a medium-sized mixing bowl, combine the eggs, maple syrup, and vanilla extract. Blend the wet ingredients with an electric hand mixer until frothy. Pour the dry ingredients into the wet ingredients and blend again until smooth.

Melt the palm shortening over medium-low heat, then allow it to cool slightly. Once the shortening has cooled, pour it into the batter and blend the batter again with the hand mixer on medium-high speed until smooth. This will allow air to be whipped into the batter slightly.

Fill each muffin cup three-quarters full with batter and bake on the middle rack of the oven until a toothpick inserted comes out clean, about 20 minutes for standard cupcakes or 10 minutes for mini cupcakes. Allow the cupcakes to cool completely.

To fill the cupcakes, fit a piping bag with a round decorating tip and fill the bag with lemon curd. Push the tip into the center of a cupcake and squeeze in the curd while simultaneously pulling the piping bag out of the cupcake. Repeat with the remaining cupcakes, filling the piping bag with more lemon curd as needed. Once the cupcakes are filled, frost them. Keep refrigerated in an airtight container, and consume within 2 days.

Cook's Notes:

We used India Tree natural food color to color the frosting yellow. Simply add food coloring until you have created the shade you like. These natural food dyes are very soft in hue, so unless you use a good amount, you will get a very pale color. We used a Wilton 230 decorating tip to fill the cupcakes and a Wilton 1M tip to frost the roses on the cupcakes.

To make this recipe dairy-free, omit the lemon curd, add the zest of 1 lemon to the batter, and frost the cupcakes with Dairy-Free Vanilla Frosting (pg 394).

maple vanilla bean ice cream

Serves: **4**   Prep time: **15 minutes, plus 30 minutes to cool**   Processing time: **20 minutes**

· Dairy-free   · Nut-free   · Egg-free   · Nightshade-free

2 (13 1/2 oz) cans full-fat coconut milk

1/2 cup granulated maple sugar

1/4 cup tapioca starch (see Note)

1 vanilla bean

Caramelized Maple Balsamic (pg 234)

Fresh blackberries, for garnish (optional)

Special equipment:

Ice cream maker

Place the coconut milk, maple sugar, and tapioca starch in a medium-sized saucepan and whisk to combine.

Slice the vanilla bean down the center and scrape the seeds into the saucepan. Whisk again to incorporate the vanilla bean seeds into the coconut milk mixture. Discard the seed pod.

Place the saucepan over medium heat and whisk the mixture continuously until steam rises and it starts to bubble slightly. Reduce the heat to medium-low and continue to whisk the mixture until it thickens, about 7–10 minutes.

Pour the thickened mixture into a heatproof glass mixing bowl. Allow the mixture to cool to room temperature, about 30 minutes.

If you are planning to serve the ice cream right away after processing, prepare the Caramelized Maple Balsamic while the ice cream mixture is chilling and set it aside.

Churn the chilled liquid in an ice cream maker according to the manufacturer's instructions. This should take about 20 minutes. Enjoy immediately for a soft-serve like texture, or place in the freezer for 2 hours to harden before serving. Serve the ice cream topped with a drizzle of the Caramelized Maple Balsamic, along with a few blackberries, if desired.

Cook's Note:

You can use 1 Tbsp plus 2 tsp of grass-fed gelatin in place of the tapioca starch in this recipe if you cannot have tapioca. If using the gelatin, allow the mixture to scald before adding the gelatin, a little bit at a time, while whisking vigorously.

meringue frosting

Yield: **enough frosting for a two-layer, 9-inch cake**   Time needed: **20 minutes**

· Dairy-free   · Nut-free   · Nightshade-free

 ❝Meringue can be tricky to make, but it's well worth the effort. The first time I made meringue frosting, I exclaimed, 'This tastes like marshmallow! It's incredible!' You'll can't help but lick the beater to sample this tasty treat. ❞

2/3 cup plus 1 Tbsp granulated maple sugar, divided

1/4 cup filtered water

Pinch of sea salt

3 large egg whites

1 1/2 tsp fresh lemon juice

Special equipment:

Candy thermometer

Place 2/3 cup of the maple sugar, water, and salt in a medium-sized saucepan over medium heat. Stir until the sugar has dissolved completely into the water. Place a candy thermometer in the sugar water and continue to heat until the temperature reaches 240°F.

While the sugar water is heating, whip the egg whites: Place the egg whites and lemon juice in a stand mixer and beat on medium speed until frothy. Add the remaining 1 Tbsp of maple sugar and beat on high speed until soft peaks form.

Turn the mixer back down to medium speed and slowly pour in the hot sugar mixture. Once the sugar is completely incorporated into the egg whites, turn the mixer back up to high speed and beat until stiff peaks form.

Cook's Note:

It is very important that you make your meringue in a cool house with low humidity. If there is any heat or humidity in the air, the meringue will not set up properly.

no-bake cinnamon cookie bites

Yield: **20 cookie bites**   Time needed: **15 minutes**

· Dairy-free   · Egg-free   · Nightshade-free

 66 These adorable no-bake cookie bites are perfect when you need just a little something sweet. They also make a great dessert for kids' school lunches. Pack them on trips for an easy snack, or bring them along to a party for a guilt-free treat for all your friends to share! 99

1/2 cup raw cashews

7 oz (1 packed cup) Medjool dates, pitted

1/2 cup unsweetened shredded coconut

1 Tbsp coconut oil, softened (see Note)

1 tsp pure vanilla extract

1 tsp ground cinnamon

In a food processor, pulse the cashews until finely chopped. Add the dates and shredded coconut and blend on high speed until a ball forms.

Press down the date mixture with a spatula. Add the coconut oil, vanilla extract, and cinnamon and purée until the ingredients are fully combined.

Scoop the date mixture into a small mixing bowl and line a 9-by-13-inch baking dish with parchment paper. Form the mixture into 1-oz balls (about 1 inch in diameter) by rolling it between your palms. Place the balls on the parchment paper and refrigerate until ready to serve. These will keep in a tightly sealed container in the refrigerator for up to 2 weeks.

Cook's Note:

If your coconut oil is cold and therefore very hard, warm it on low heat in a small saucepan until it is soft enough that it will blend well into the cookie mixture. It does not need to be melted to a liquid.

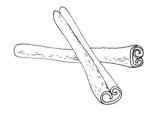

nut-free pie/tart crust

Yield: **one 9-inch crust**   Prep time: **15 minutes**   Cook time: **20 minutes**

· Dairy-free   · Nut-free   · Nightshade-free

1/2 cup (63 grams) coconut flour

1/2 cup (55 grams) arrowroot starch

1/2 cup (75 grams) granulated maple sugar

1/4 tsp sea salt

2 large eggs

1 tsp pure vanilla extract

1 Tbsp coconut oil, melted, plus more for the pan

Preheat the oven to 325°F. Lightly grease a 9-inch pie pan or tart pan with coconut oil.

Place the coconut flour, arrowroot starch, maple sugar, and salt in a small mixing bowl and stir to combine.

In another small bowl, whisk the eggs and vanilla extract until frothy. Pour the egg mixture into the flour mixture and stir to combine. Add the melted coconut oil and stir until the eggs and coconut milk are fully incorporated into the flour.

Work the dough with your hands, carefully pressing it evenly into the greased pan. Bake for 20 minutes, until cooked through and slightly golden. Allow the crust to cool, then fill with the desired sweet pie filling.

graham cracker pie/tart crust

Yield: **one 9-inch crust**   Prep time: **15 minutes**   Cook time: **15 minutes**

· Dairy-free   · Nightshade-free

1 cup (105 grams) blanched almond flour

1/2 cup (56 grams) chestnut flour

1/2 cup (55 grams) arrowroot starch

1 tsp ground cinnamon

1/4 tsp sea salt

1 large egg

1 tsp pure vanilla extract

1 Tbsp coconut oil, melted, plus more for the pan

2 Tbsp cold filtered water

Preheat the oven to 325°F. Lightly grease a 9-inch pie pan or tart pan with coconut oil.

Place the almond flour, chestnut flour, arrowroot starch, cinnamon, and salt in a small mixing bowl and stir to combine.

In another small bowl, whisk the egg and vanilla extract until frothy. Pour the egg mixture into the flour mixture and stir to combine. Add the melted coconut oil and stir until the egg and coconut oil are fully incorporated into the flour.

Mix in the cold water. When the dough is an even consistency, carefully press it evenly into the greased pan. Bake for 15 minutes, until cooked through and slightly golden. Allow the crust to cool, then fill with the desired sweet pie filling.

petite chocolate cake

Yield: **one two-layer, 6-inch cake**   Prep time: **25 minutes**   Cook time: **35–45 minutes**

· Dairy-free   · Nut-free   · Nightshade-free

❝Petite cakes are my favorite. I love anything in a mini size, and a miniature cake is just adorable. Perfect for a bridal or baby shower, this cake packs big flavor in a small package. ❞

1/2 cup palm shortening

1/2 cup (63 grams) coconut flour

1/2 cup (60 grams) tapioca starch

1/2 cup (36 grams) cocoa powder

1 tsp Baking Powder (pg 274)

1/2 tsp sea salt

6 large eggs

3/4 cup pure maple syrup

1 tsp pure vanilla extract

Dairy-Free Vanilla Frosting (pg 394)

Sliced fresh strawberries, for garnish (optional)

Preheat the oven to 350°F. Liberally grease two 6-inch springform cake pans and place them on a small baking sheet.

Melt the palm shortening in a small saucepan over medium-low heat. Once melted, remove from the heat and set aside.

In a small mixing bowl, stir together the coconut flour, tapioca starch, cocoa powder, baking powder, and salt until blended. In a medium-sized mixing bowl, beat the eggs, maple syrup, and vanilla extract with an electric hand mixer. Sift the dry mixture into the wet mixture and beat again with the hand mixer until the batter is smooth.

Pour in the cooled palm shortening and beat again until the batter is smooth and creamy. Let it sit for about 5 minutes, until the coconut flour absorbs some of the moisture in the batter, then beat again with the hand mixer to add slightly more air to the batter.

Pour the batter evenly into the two prepared pans. Bake on the middle rack of the oven for 35–45 minutes, until a toothpick inserted comes out clean. While the cakes are baking, make the frosting.

Allow the cakes to cool completely in the pans, then remove by releasing the clasps and running an offset spatula underneath to release each cake from its base. Frost, then garnish with strawberries, if desired. The frosted cake will keep in the fridge for up to 4–5 days.

Variation: Chocolate Cupcakes

You can also use this batter to make cupcakes. Line a standard muffin tin with paper liners and fill the cups using a standard-size ice cream scoop (2 oz). Bake the cupcakes at 350°F for 20 minutes, until a toothpick inserted comes out clean, and frost once cooled. Makes 1 dozen.

Cook's Notes:

Coconut flour tends to absorb moisture from the cake. To keep these cakes moist if you are not frosting and serving them right away, store them at room temperature, wrapping both layers in plastic wrap. Remove the plastic wrap right before frosting and serving. Store the cakes this way for up to 24 hours before frosting. If you are not serving the cake directly after frosting it, keep it refrigerated so that the frosting stays chilled.

snickerdoodles

Yield: **20 cookies**   Prep time: **15 minutes**   Cook time: **40 minutes**

· Dairy-free   · Nightshade-free

1 Tbsp granulated maple sugar

1 tsp ground cinnamon

2 cups (216 grams) blanched almond flour

1/2 cup (56 grams) chestnut flour

1 tsp Baking Powder (pg 274)

1/2 tsp sea salt

2 large eggs

1/2 cup pure maple syrup

1 tsp pure vanilla extract

1/4 cup palm shortening

Preheat the oven to 350°F. Line two baking sheets with parchment paper.

Combine the maple sugar and cinnamon in a small mixing bowl and set aside.

Combine the almond flour, chestnut flour, baking powder, and salt in a medium-sized mixing bowl. In a small bowl, blend the eggs, maple syrup, and vanilla extract with an electric hand mixer.

In a small saucepan over low heat, warm the palm shortening until it is almost completely melted. Remove from the heat and allow to cool.

Pour the egg mixture into the dry ingredients and blend with the hand mixer until smooth. Pour the cooled palm shortening into the dough and blend again until smooth.

Using a #50 cookie scoop or two spoons, scoop 1 1/4-Tbsp portions of the dough onto the lined baking sheets. Grease your hands with palm shortening or coconut oil and lightly press the cookies down with your palms to form even, round cookie shapes.

Sprinkle the cookies with the maple sugar and cinnamon mixture. Bake each sheet on the middle rack of the oven for 20 minutes, until cooked through and golden on the edges. Allow to cool before serving. Keep the cookies in a tightly sealed container in the refrigerator for up to 1 week, or freeze for longer storage.

stracciatella gelato

Serves: **4**   Prep time: **20 minutes, plus 30 minutes to cool**   Processing time: **20 minutes**

· Dairy-free   · Nut-free   · Egg-free   · Nightshade-free

2 (13 1/2-oz) cans full-fat coconut milk

1/2 cup granulated maple sugar

1/4 cup tapioca starch

2 tsp pure vanilla extract

1/3 cup allergen-free dark chocolate chips

1 tsp coconut oil

CHOCOLATE SHELL
(optional; see Note)

1/3 cup allergen-free dark chocolate chips

1 tsp coconut oil

Special equipment:

Ice cream maker

Place the coconut milk, maple sugar, tapioca starch, and vanilla extract in a medium-sized saucepan. Whisk to combine the ingredients.

Once the tapioca starch is completely incorporated into the milk, place the pan over medium heat and heat the milk mixture, whisking constantly, until steam rises. Reduce the heat to medium-low and continue to whisk until the mixture thickens, 7–10 minutes.

Once the mixture has thickened, remove from the heat, pour into a mixing bowl, and allow to cool to room temperature, about 30 minutes.

Once the mixture has cooled completely, melt the chocolate chips and coconut oil in a small saucepan over low heat, stirring. Allow the chocolate to cool while the ice cream is churning.

Churn the chilled liquid in an ice cream maker according to the manufacturer's instructions. This should take about 20 minutes.

At the 19-minute mark of processing, slowly drizzle the melted chocolate in a very thin stream over the ice cream to create small chips of chocolate throughout the ice cream. Once all of the chocolate is added, allow the ice cream to churn for about 30–60 seconds to make sure that the chocolate is mixed in evenly.

Enjoy immediately for a soft-serve like texture, or place in the freezer for 2–4 hours to harden before serving.

Cook's Note:

To make the chocolate shell, repeat the instructions for making the chocolate drizzle in the fourth step above. Drizzle this melted chocolate over the ice cream just before serving. It will form a shell in about a minute.

vanilla buttercream frosting

Yield: **1 1/2 cups**   Time needed: **20 minutes**

· Nut-free   · Egg-free   · Nightshade-free

1 cup (2 sticks) unsalted grass-fed butter, room temperature

1 Tbsp full-fat coconut milk or grass-fed heavy cream

1 tsp pure vanilla extract

1 1/2 cups powdered sugar, store-bought or homemade (pg 292), sifted (see Notes)

Natural food coloring of choice (optional)

Place the butter in a stand mixer. Using the flat beater attachment, whip the butter on high speed until it is fluffy and light in color, about 5 minutes. You may need to scrape down the sides of the bowl every so often.

Add the coconut milk and vanilla extract and beat on high speed for 3 minutes. Turn the mixer off and add the powdered sugar, a little at a time, beating on medium speed after each addition of sugar. Scrape down the sides of the bowl as needed. Once all of the sugar is added and the frosting is whipped smooth, add the food coloring, if desired. Use immediately or refrigerate for up to 4 days.

dairy-free vanilla frosting

Yield: **2 1/2 cups**   Time needed: **10 minutes**

· Dairy-free   · Nut-free   · Egg-free   · Nightshade-free

2 cups palm shortening

2/3 cup powdered sugar, store-bought or homemade (pg 292)

1 tsp pure vanilla extract

Natural food coloring of choice (optional)

Scoop the palm shortening into a medium-sized mixing bowl. Sift in the powdered sugar, then beat with an electric hand mixer until smooth and fluffy.

Add the vanilla extract and beat again until the frosting is completely smooth and fluffy. Add the food coloring, if desired. Use immediately or refrigerate for up to 1 week.

Cook's Notes:

When we want to make cupcakes or a cake for a birthday or other special occasion, we sweeten our vanilla frosting with organic powdered sugar that does not contain cornstarch. The Powdered Sugar recipe on pg 292 will work just as well, but because it is made from maple sugar, it will color the frosting tan. If you would like to color your frosting, you must use white sugar because natural food coloring is not strong enough to overcome the maple sugar color. The photo shows our vanilla frosting made with organic white powdered sugar.

The dairy-free version of this frosting has a softer consistency. It is not sturdy enough for piping decorations onto cakes or cupcakes.

wedding cake

Yield: **one two-layer, 6-inch cake**   Prep time: **20 minutes**   Cook time: **40–45 minutes**

• Dairy-free   • Nightshade-free

Lemon Curd (pg 376), for filling

Meringue Frosting (pg 382) or Dairy-Free Vanilla Frosting (pg 394)

1/2 cup palm shortening, plus more for the pans

1 1/4 cups (125 grams) blanched almond flour

1/4 cup (32 grams) coconut flour

3/4 cup (110 grams) granulated maple sugar

2 tsp Baking Powder (pg 274)

1/2 tsp sea salt

3 large eggs

1/2 cup full-fat coconut milk

1 tsp pure vanilla extract

Fresh berries of choice (halved or quartered if large), for filling

Make the lemon curd and place in the refrigerator to chill. While the curd is chilling, make the frosting and set aside until needed.

Preheat the oven to 350°F. Liberally grease two 6-inch springform cake pans or one standard 9-inch cake pan (see Notes).

Melt the palm shortening in a small saucepan over medium-low heat, then set it aside to cool slightly.

In a large mixing bowl, sift together the almond flour, coconut flour, maple sugar, baking powder, and salt. In a medium-sized mixing bowl, blend the eggs, coconut milk, and vanilla extract with an electric hand mixer. Add the wet ingredients to the dry ingredients and blend again with the hand mixer until the batter is smooth.

Add the cooled palm shortening to the batter and beat again until smooth.

Pour the batter into two 6-inch cake pans or one 9-inch cake pan. Bake on the middle rack of the oven for 40–45 minutes, until a toothpick inserted comes out clean. Allow to cool completely in the pans before frosting.

Place one cake layer on a cake plate or stand. Evenly spread the lemon curd on top of the cake layer and arrange berries of your choice on top. Place the second cake layer on top and frost the top and sides of the cake.

Cook's Notes:

If using a 9-inch cake pan, you can serve this cake as a single frosted layer, topped with fresh berries and with the lemon curd on the side. You can also double the batter recipe to make two 9-inch cakes to create a two-layer cake in the larger size.

Springform cake pans work best for cakes because they ensure that your cakes come out of the pans looking beautiful and fully intact. If you are using a regular cake pan, be sure to grease it liberally before baking, and run a butter knife around the edge before removing the cake. To remove the cake, place a plate over the top of the pan and flip, then carefully slide the cake onto a cake stand for decorating.

whipped coconut cream

Yield: **3 cups**   Prep time: **10 minutes, plus 8–10 hours to chill the coconut milk**

· Dairy-free   · Nut-free   · Egg-free   · Nightshade-free

 66 Whipped Coconut Cream is an easy treat that can be used as a frosting for cakes and cupcakes, used as a topping for pies, or simply enjoyed with a small bowl of fresh berries. 99

2 (13 1/2-oz) cans full-fat coconut milk

2 tsp raw honey or 12–15 drops of liquid stevia extract

1 tsp pure vanilla extract

Place the cans of coconut milk in the refrigerator to chill overnight, or for at least 8 hours.

When you're ready to make the Whipped Coconut Cream, place a small stainless-steel mixing bowl in the freezer to chill for 5 minutes.

Remove the bowl from the freezer and remove the cans of coconut milk from the fridge. Open the cans of coconut milk from the bottom, scoop the thick cream off the top, and place the cream in the chilled mixing bowl. Add the honey and vanilla extract. Using an electric hand mixer or stand mixer, whip on high speed until fluffy, about 3–5 minutes.

Place the Whipped Coconut Cream back in the fridge to stiffen up if you plan to pipe it onto a pie, cake, or cupcakes.

simple raspberry parfaits

Serves: **2**   Time needed: **5 minutes**

· Dairy-free   · Egg-free   · Nightshade-free

8 oz fresh raspberries (just over 1 cup)

1/4 cup chopped raw walnuts

2 cups Whipped Coconut Cream (above)

Layer some raspberries and chopped walnuts in the bottom of each of two small dessert glasses. Top with some Whipped Coconut Cream.

Repeat this process, creating a second layer of berries and nuts and a second layer of whipped cream.

resources

pack a picnic

116
chicken salad with currants

124
honey sesame wings

202
cold sesame zoodles

208
mango and avocado salad

222
smoky slaw

220
roasted sweet potatoes with citrus dressing

316
sangria

370
grain-free fudgy brownies

birthday party

388
petite chocolate cake

378
luscious lemon cupcakes

320
cauliflower crust vegetable pizza

310
natural soda syrups

338
zucchini fritters

144
thai fried chicken with tangy mango sauce

take out, stay in

96 pork dumplings

128 orange chicken

156 ginger suimono

230 vegetable lo mein

176 spicy tuna dip

322 fried wontons

easy brunch

374 lemon blueberry waffles

342 apple streusel muffins

206 home fries

68 breakfast casserole

88 nightshade-free breakfast sausage

summer BBQ

74

dry-rubbed
spareribs

154

fish tacos with
smoky slaw

228

sweet potato fries
with homemade
ketchup

70

burgers with pork belly,
roasted red peppers,
and spicy aioli

220

roasted sweet
potatoes with
citrus dressing

314

raspberry lemonade

366

double chocolate
chip cookies

comfort food

226

stuffed acorn squash

120

chicken zoodle soup
with meatballs

200

celery root puree

218

roasted potatoes,
carrots, and celery

390

snickerdoodles

306

hot cocoa

tex mex

72

carne asada with
pico de gallo

80

lamb barbacoa tacos

316

sangria

154

fish tacos with
smoky slaw

334

tortillas

beach days

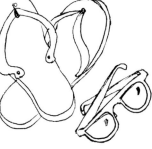

168

scallop ceviche

166

santorini
seafood stew

158

lobster and
avocado salad

198

cauliflower couscous

344

berry and ginger
granita

holiday dinner

164
salmon cakes
with garlic-chive aioli

152
creamy crab bisque

196
caramelized fennel
with sweet potato
puree

134
roasted cornish
game hens

190
beet and
goat cheese salad

218
roasted potatoes,
carrots, and celery

356
chocolate
pudding pie

italian night

210
minestrone

160
lobster fettuccine
alfredo

326
nightshade-free
pizza

212
oven-roasted
summer vegetables
with herbs

392
stracciatella gelato

table for two

82

lamb chops with maple balsamic glaze

194

caramelized carrots

214

poached pear salad with crispy shallots and caramelized maple balsamic

212

oven-roasted summer vegetables with herbs

308

moscow mule

398

simple raspberry parfaits

dietary restriction index

meat

	Dairy-free	Nut-free	Egg-free	Nightshade-free
beef daube (pg 60)	no*	yes	yes	no
braised beef heart (pg 62)	no*	yes	yes	no
braised lamb shanks (pg 64)	no*	yes	yes	no
breakfast beef hash (pg 66)	yes	yes	yes	no
breakfast casserole (pg 68)	yes	yes	no	no
burgers with pork belly, roasted red peppers, and spicy aioli (pg 70)	yes	no	no	no
carne asada with pico de gallo (pg 72)	yes	yes	yes	no
dry-rubbed spareribs (pg 74)	yes	yes	yes	no
empanadas (pg 76)	yes	no	no	no
grilled sirloin skewers (pg 78)	yes	yes	yes	no
lamb barbacoa tacos (pg 80)	yes	yes	no	no
lamb chops with maple balsamic glaze (pg 82)	no	yes	yes	yes
lamb gyros with tzatziki sauce (pg 84)	no*	yes	no	no*
moroccan short ribs (pg 86)	yes	yes	yes	no
nightshade-free breakfast sausage (pg 88)	yes	yes	yes	yes
porcini-crusted lamb chops (pg 90)	yes	yes	yes	yes
pork and apple ravioli (pg 92)	yes	no	no	no
pork chops with apple chutney (pg 94)	yes	yes	yes	no
pork dumplings (pg 96)	yes	no	no	no
pork meatballs with creamy sauce (pg 98)	yes	yes	yes	no
ramen with chashu and marinated eggs (pg 100)	yes	yes	no	yes
scottish meat pies (pg 104)	no	no	no	no
smoked ribs (pg 106)	yes	yes	yes	no

poultry & eggs

	Dairy-free	Nut-free	Egg-free	Nightshade-free
asian chicken salad (pg 110)	yes	no*	no	yes
baked eggs with spaghetti squash (pg 112)	yes	yes	no	no
chicken en brodo (pg 114)	yes	yes	yes	yes
chicken salad with currants (pg 116)	yes	no	no	no
chicken salsa salad (pg 118)	yes	yes	yes	no
chicken zoodle soup with meatballs (pg 120)	yes	yes	yes	yes
hash brown nested eggs (pg 122)	yes	yes	no	yes
honey sesame wings (pg 124)	yes	yes	yes	no*
lemongrass chicken curry (pg 126)	yes	yes	yes	no
orange chicken (pg 128)	yes	yes	no	no
pesto pasta with chicken (pg 130)	yes	no*	yes	no

no* — optional modification

	Dairy-free	Nut-free	Egg-free	Nightshade-free
roasted chicken with aromatic spices (pg 132)	yes	yes	yes	no
roasted cornish game hens (pg 134)	yes	yes	yes	yes
skillet chicken thighs (pg 136)	yes	yes	yes	yes
spinach and artichoke quiche (pg 138)	yes	no	no	yes
stuffed chicken thighs (pg 140)	yes	yes	yes	no
summer spring rolls with "peanut" sauce (pg 142)	yes	yes	yes	no*
thai fried chicken with tangy mango sauce (pg 144)	yes	yes	no	no*
tortilla española (pg 146)	yes	yes	no	yes

seafood

	Dairy-free	Nut-free	Egg-free	Nightshade-free
clam chowder (pg 150)	no*	yes	yes	no
creamy crab bisque (pg 152)	no*	yes	yes	no
fish tacos with smoky slaw (pg 154)	yes	yes	no	no
ginger suimono (pg 156)	yes	yes	yes	yes
lobster and avocado salad (pg 158)	yes	yes	yes	yes
lobster fettuccine alfredo (pg 160)	yes	no*	yes	no*
pan-seared salmon with avocado "cream" sauce (pg 162)	yes	yes	yes	yes
salmon cakes with garlic-chive aioli (pg 164)	yes	no*	no	no
santorini seafood stew (pg 166)	yes	yes	yes	no
scallop ceviche (pg 168)	yes	yes	yes	no
shrimp, avocado, and grapefruit salad (pg 170)	no*	yes	yes	yes
shrimp and scallop scampi (pg 172)	yes	yes	no	yes
smoked flounder hand rolls (pg 174)	yes	yes	no	yes
spicy tuna dip (pg 176)	yes	yes	no	no
whole roasted mackerel (pg 178)	yes	yes	yes	yes

plants

	Dairy-free	Nut-free	Egg-free	Nightshade-free
apple bacon butternut squash soup (pg 182)	no*	yes	yes	yes
baby broccoli with bacon (pg 184)	yes	yes	yes	yes
bacon and yellow squash hash (pg 186)	yes	yes	no	yes
basic cauliflower rice (pg 188)	yes	yes	yes	yes
beet and goat cheese salad (pg 190)	no	no	yes	no
braised brussels sprouts (pg 192)	yes	yes	yes	yes
caramelized carrots (pg 194)	no	yes	yes	yes
caramelized fennel with sweet potato puree (pg 196)	no*	yes	yes	yes
cauliflower couscous (pg 198)	yes	no	yes	no

no* — optional modification

	Dairy-free	Nut-free	Egg-free	Nightshade-free
celery root puree (pg 200)	no*	yes	yes	yes
cold sesame zoodles (pg 202)	yes	yes	yes	no
ethiopian cabbage (pg 204)	yes	yes	yes	yes
home fries (pg 206)	yes	yes	yes	no
mango and avocado salad (pg 208)	yes	yes	yes	no*
minestrone (pg 210)	no*	yes	yes	no
oven-roasted summer vegetables with herbs (pg 212)	yes	yes	yes	no
poached pear salad with crispy shallots and caramelized maple balsamic (pg 214)	no*	yes	yes	yes
roasted head of cauliflower (pg 216)	yes	yes	yes	yes
roasted potatoes, carrots, and celery (pg 218)	yes	yes	yes	no
roasted sweet potatoes with citrus dressing (pg 220)	yes	yes	yes	yes
smoky slaw (pg 222)	yes	yes	no	no
spiced cranberry relish (pg 224)	yes	yes	yes	yes
stuffed acorn squash (pg 226)	yes	yes	yes	yes
sweet potato fries with homemade ketchup (pg 228)	yes	yes	yes	no
vegetable lo mein (pg 230)	yes	yes	yes	no*

sauces & dressings

	Dairy-free	Nut-free	Egg-free	Nightshade-free
caramelized maple balsamic (pg 234)	yes	yes	yes	yes
cilantro ginger dressing (pg 236)	yes	yes	yes	yes
citrus vinaigrette (pg 238)	yes	yes	yes	no*
dumpling sauce (pg 240)	yes	yes	yes	no
garlic-chive aioli (pg 242)	yes	no*	no	yes
homemade mayonnaise (pg 244)	yes	yes	no	yes
lemon-caper aioli (pg 246)	yes	yes	no	yes
lemon vinaigrette (pg 248)	yes	yes	yes	yes
oyster sauce (pg 250)	yes	yes	yes	yes
"peanut" sauce (pg 252)	yes	yes	yes	no
pico de gallo (pg 254)	yes	yes	yes	no
pizza sauce (pg 256)	yes	yes	yes	no
red sauce with a kick (pg 258)	yes	yes	yes	no
roasted zucchini aioli (pg 260)	yes	yes	no	yes
smoky barbecue sauce (pg 262)	yes	yes	yes	no
tangy mango sauce (pg 264)	yes	yes	yes	no
tzatziki (pg 266)	no*	yes	yes	yes
walnut pesto (pg 268)	yes	no	yes	yes
nut-free pesto (pg 268)	yes	yes	yes	yes

no* — optional modification

basics & projects

	Dairy-free	Nut-free	Egg-free	Nightshade-free
baking powder (pg 274)	yes	yes	yes	yes
cherry vanilla coconut milk yogurt (pg 276)	yes	yes	yes	yes
chicken stock and beef stock (pg 278)	yes	yes	yes	yes
cured bacon (pg 280)	yes	yes	yes	yes
cured salmon (pg 282)	yes	yes	yes	yes
dashi (pg 284)	yes	yes	yes	yes
ghee (pg 286)	yes	yes	yes	yes
ginger beer (pg 288)	yes	yes	yes	yes
pickled burdock root (pg 290)	yes	yes	yes	no
powdered sugar (pg 292)	yes	yes	yes	yes
rendered lard (pg 294)	yes	yes	yes	yes
tomato jam (pg 296)	no*	yes	yes	no

drinks

	Dairy-free	Nut-free	Egg-free	Nightshade-free
basic nut milk (pg 300)	yes	no	yes	yes
chocolate banana milkshake (pg 302)	yes	no	yes	yes
coconut milk cortado (pg 304)	yes	yes	yes	yes
hot cocoa (pg 306)	yes	yes	yes	yes
moscow mule (pg 308)	yes	yes	yes	yes
natural soda syrups (pg 310)	yes	yes	yes	yes
pumpkin spice latte (pg 312)	yes	no	yes	yes
raspberry lemonade (pg 314)	yes	yes	yes	yes
sangria (pg 316)	yes	yes	yes	yes

savory things

	Dairy-free	Nut-free	Egg-free	Nightshade-free
cauliflower crust vegetable pizza (pg 320)	no	yes	no	no
fried wontons (pg 322)	yes	no*	no	yes
grain-free sandwich bread (pg 324)	yes	no	no	no
nightshade-free pizza (pg 326)	yes	yes	no	yes
nut-free pasta dough (pg 328)	yes	yes	no	yes
quiche crust (pg 330)	yes	no	no	yes
savory chestnut flour pie crusts (pg 332)	yes	no	no	yes
tortillas (pg 334)	yes	yes	no	yes
wrapper dough (pg 336)	yes	no*	no	yes
zucchini fritters (pg 338)	yes	yes	no	yes

no* — optional modification

sweet things

	Dairy-free	Nut-free	Egg-free	Nightshade-free
apple streusel muffins (pg 342)	yes	no	no	yes
berry and ginger granita (pg 344)	yes	yes	yes	yes
blueberry tart (pg 346)	yes	yes	no	yes
chocolate chip sunbutter cookies (pg 348)	yes	yes	no	yes
chocolate-covered bacon (pg 350)	yes	yes	yes	yes
chocolate fruit and nut bars (pg 352)	yes	no	yes	yes
chocolate "peanut butter" squares (pg 354)	yes	no*	yes	yes
chocolate pudding pie (pg 356)	yes	no*	no	yes
chocolate sunbutter cups (pg 358)	yes	yes	yes	yes
cranberry hand pies (pg 360)	yes	no	no	yes
dairy-free chocolate mousse (pg 362)	yes	yes	yes	yes
dark chocolate, olive oil, and sea salt ice cream (pg 364)	yes	yes	yes	yes
double chocolate chip cookies (pg 366)	yes	no	no	yes
fluffy dairy-free chocolate frosting (pg 368)	yes	yes	yes	yes
grain-free fudgy brownies (pg 370)	yes	no	no	yes
granola two ways (pg 372)	yes	no	yes	yes
lemon blueberry waffles (pg 374)	yes	yes	no	yes
lemon curd (pg 376)	no	yes	no	yes
luscious lemon cupcakes (pg 378)	no*	yes	no	yes
maple vanilla bean ice cream (pg 380)	yes	yes	yes	yes
meringue frosting (pg 382)	yes	yes	no	yes
no-bake cinnamon cookie bites (pg 384)	yes	no	yes	yes
nut-free pie/tart crust (pg 386)	yes	yes	no	yes
graham cracker pie/tart crust (pg 386)	yes	no	no	yes
petite chocolate cake (pg 388)	yes	yes	no	yes
snickerdoodles (pg 390)	yes	no	no	yes
stracciatella gelato (pg 392)	yes	yes	yes	yes
vanilla buttercream frosting (pg 394)	no	yes	yes	yes
dairy-free vanilla frosting (pg 394)	yes	yes	yes	yes
wedding cake (pg 396)	yes	no	no	yes
whipped coconut cream (pg 398)	yes	yes	yes	yes
simple raspberry parfaits (pg 398)	yes	no	yes	yes

no* — optional modification

Luscious Lemon Cupcakes

3/4 c. arrowroot starch

1/2 c. coconut flour

1/2 tsp. sea salt

1/4 tsp. baking soda

6 large eggs

1/2 c. pure maple syrup

2 tsp. vanilla extract

1/4 c. palm shortening

· Lemon Curd

· Vanilla Buttercream

recipe index

meat

60
beef daube

62
braised beef heart

64
braised lamb shanks

66
breakfast beef hash

68
breakfast casserole

70
burgers with pork belly, roasted red peppers, and spicy aioli

72
carne asada with pico de gallo

74
dry-rubbed spareribs

76
empanadas

78
grilled sirloin skewers

80
lamb barbacoa tacos

82
lamb chops with maple balsamic glaze

84
lamb gyros with tzatziki sauce

86
moroccan short ribs

88
nightshade-free breakfast sausage

90
porcini-crusted lamb chops

92
pork and apple ravioli

94
pork chops with apple chutney

96
pork dumplings

98
pork meatballs with creamy sauce

100
ramen with chashu and marinated eggs

104
scottish meat pies

106
smoked ribs

poultry & eggs

110 asian chicken salad

112 baked eggs with spaghetti squash

114 chicken en brodo

116 chicken salad with currants

118 chicken salsa salad

120 chicken zoodle soup with meatballs

122 hash brown nested eggs

124 honey sesame wings

126 lemongrass chicken curry

128 orange chicken

130 pesto pasta with chicken

132 roasted chicken with aromatic spices

134 roasted cornish game hens

136 skillet chicken thighs

138 spinach and artichoke quiche

140 stuffed chicken thighs

142 summer spring rolls with "peanut" sauce

144 thai fried chicken with tangy mango sauce

146 tortilla española

seafood

150

clam chowder

152

creamy crab bisque

154

fish tacos with
smoky slaw

156

ginger suimono

158

lobster and
avocado salad

160

lobster fettuccine
alfredo

162

pan-seared salmon
with avocado
"cream" sauce

164

salmon cakes
with garlic-chive aioli

166

santorini
seafood stew

168

scallop ceviche

170

shrimp, avocado,
and grapefruit salad

172

shrimp and scallop
scampi

174

smoked flounder
hand rolls

176

spicy tuna dip

178

whole roasted
mackerel

plants

182

apple bacon butternut squash soup

184

baby broccoli with bacon

186

bacon and yellow squash hash

188

basic cauliflower rice

190

beet and goat cheese salad

192

braised brussels sprouts

194

caramelized carrots

196

caramelized fennel with sweet potato puree

198

cauliflower couscous

200

celery root puree

202

cold sesame zoodles

204

ethiopian cabbage

206

home fries

208

mango and avocado salad

210

minestrone

212

oven-roasted summer vegetables with herbs

214

poached pear salad with crispy shallots and caramelized maple balsamic

216

roasted head of cauliflower

218

roasted potatoes, carrots, and celery

220

roasted sweet potatoes with citrus dressing

222

smoky slaw

224

spiced cranberry relish

226

stuffed acorn squash

228

sweet potato fries with homemade ketchup

230

vegetable lo mein

sauces & dressings

234
caramelized maple balsamic

236
cilantro ginger dressing

238
citrus vinaigrette

240
dumpling sauce

242
garlic-chive aioli

244
homemade mayonnaise

246
lemon-caper aioli

248
lemon vinaigrette

250
oyster sauce

252
"peanut" sauce

254
pico de gallo

256
pizza sauce

258
red sauce with a kick

260
roasted zucchini aioli

262
smoky barbecue sauce

264
tangy mango sauce

266
tzatziki

268
walnut pesto & nut-free pesto

basics & projects

272

10 spice blends

274

baking powder

276

cherry vanilla
coconut milk yogurt

278

chicken stock
and beef stock

280

cured bacon

282

cured salmon

284

dashi

286

ghee

288

ginger beer

290

pickled burdock root

292

powdered sugar

294

rendered lard

296

tomato jam

drinks

300 basic nut milk

302 chocolate banana milkshake

304 coconut milk cortado

306 hot cocoa

308 moscow mule

310 natural soda syrups

312 pumpkin spice latte

314 raspberry lemonade

316 sangria

savory things

320 cauliflower crust vegetable pizza

322 fried wontons

324 grain-free sandwich bread

326 nightshade-free pizza

328 nut-free pasta dough

330 quiche crust

332 savory chestnut flour pie crusts

334 tortillas

336 wrapper dough

338 zucchini fritters

sweet things

342
apple streusel muffins

344
berry and ginger granita

346
blueberry tart

348
chocolate chip sunbutter cookies

350
chocolate-covered bacon

352
chocolate fruit and nut bars

354
chocolate "peanut butter" squares

356
chocolate pudding pie

358
chocolate sunbutter cups

360
cranberry hand pies

362
dairy-free chocolate mousse

364
dark chocolate, olive oil, and sea salt ice cream

366
double chocolate chip cookies

368
fluffy dairy-free chocolate frosting

370
grain-free fudgy brownies

372
granola two ways

374
lemon blueberry waffles

376
lemon curd

378
luscious lemon cupcakes

380
maple vanilla bean ice cream

382
meringue frosting

384
no-bake cinnamon cookie bites

386
nut-free pie/tart crust

386
graham cracker pie/ tart crust

388
petite chocolate cake

390

snickerdoodles

392

stracciatella gelato

394

vanilla frosting

396

wedding cake

398

whipped coconut cream

398

simple raspberry parfaits

index